EDMUND BURKE

EDMUND BURKE
His Political Philosophy

Frank O'Gorman

INDIANA UNIVERSITY PRESS
Bloomington & London

Published in the United States by Indiana University Press,
and in the United Kingdom and Commonwealth countries by Allen & Unwin Ltd.
No part of this book may be reproduced or utilized in any form
or by any means, electronic or mechanical, including photocopying
and recording, or by any information storage and retrieval system,
without permission in writing from the publisher. The Association
of American University Presses Resolution on Permissions constitutes
the only exception to this prohibition.

Library of Congress catalog card number: 73-81715

ISBN: 0-253-31910-2

Manufactured in the United States of America

To My Mother

CONTENTS

EDMUND BURKE

INTRODUCTION

Edmund Burke enjoyed a remarkable historical reputation in nineteenth-century Britain. Although his contemporaries had recognized him as a philosopher, politician and statesman the Victorians saw Burke as a towering hero who had rallied his countrymen to the cause of counter-revolution, saved the constitution of Britain and the empire and moulded the Victorian system of government. They believed that his campaign against the corrupting effects of royal influence inaugurated the constitutional monarchy of the mid-nineteenth century. They admired his endeavours to establish government by party as an anticipation of the two party system of that period. In these, and in many other ways, too, Burke appeared to possess a certain prophetic quality of mind, an almost superhuman instinct for perceiving the direction in which history was about to move.

Some reaction against the fulsome praise of the Victorians, was inevitable. In the first half of this century it came and with it, the waning of Burke's reputation. Detailed examination of his career and minute analysis of the political system of the second half of the eighteenth century revealed that Burke was very much a man of his time in his ready acceptance of the political assumptions and institutions of his contemporaries. Far from being a prophet of the liberal constitution of the next century Burke sought to *restore* the old Whig constitution established at the Glorious Revolution, and which he accused George III and some of his advisors of violating. It was never Burke's intention to fashion novel political forms which anticipated the future development of the constitution. He wished to defend and protect the aristocratic world of eighteenth-century politics, an objective towards which his reforms were uniformly directed. He was too much involved in the political struggles of his own day to concern himself with the future development of the British constitution. Indeed, Edmund Burke was not a philosopher at all. He was essentially a practical politician and a propagandist rather than a thinker with a systematic philosophy to expound. His political objectives had their origin less in his own thought than in his membership of the Rockingham Whig party and his close personal relationship with the Marquis of Rockingham himself.[1] Partisanship and prejudice were evidently

---

[1] Charles, 2nd Marquis of Rockingham (1739–82) was one of the greatest Whig politicians of the age. He was Prime Minister and First Lord of the Treasury in the two short ministries of 1765–66 and 1782. He was a great Yorkshire landowner and one of the foremost electoral patrons of the day.

just as important in shaping Burke's thought as a concern for justice or impartial inquiry.[2] The awe-inspiring figure of the nineteenth century had become the party hack of the twentieth.

The pendulum of reputation soon swung over to the opposite extreme. After the Second World War there took place both a revival of interest in his work and a considerable shift in the interpretation of his thought. The revival was caused by the opening to scholars of Burke's private papers; the shift was accomplished by the American 'new conservatives' of the 1950s, upon whom Burke's influence was considerable. They saw Burke as a christian philosopher, striving to combat the evils of atheistic Jacobinism by reaffirming the traditional religious and social principles of European civilization. Regarding themselves similarly, as the Christian philosophers of the mid-twentieth century, striving to preserve the west from the infection of atheistic communism, the 'new conservatives' believed that Burke's philosophy was rooted in the christian ethic. They pointed to the central and unifying principle of his philosophy, the Natural Law, which rendered his thought both intelligible and coherent and from which it logically flowed.[3] The Natural Law does indeed enjoy a place in Burke's thought.

Rockingham was not only one of Burke's closest friends. He was his protector and patron. Burke owed his political career to the Marquis.

[2] This is *not* to say that Burke deliberately falsified facts, still less that he was consciously and deliberately self-interested. Edmund Burke hated cruelty, injustice and oppression and his whole career manifested an extraordinary elevation of the human spirit. Nevertheless, it is idle to ignore the simple fact that Burke was a politician and thus involved in the political controversies of his day. Impartial detachment could scarcely be expected from a man in Burke's position. Furthermore, Burke was a man whose entire personality inclined towards commitment rather than towards detachment. He was a man of considerable passion, trained in the law, enjoying extensive knowledge of economics, history, aesthetics, philosophy, languages and the arts. Edmund Burke was immensely fertile in ideas which flowed from him almost uncontrollably. Such a man was not inclined to abstract, rational philosophy.

[3] The Natural Law school makes at least two sorts of statement about Burke which require the exercise of caution. The first is that his thought 'developed, deepened and found new applications' (R. Hoffman and B. Levack, eds. *Burke's Politics* (New York, 1949), xiii). The second assumes that 'it seems now to have become generally recognized that Burke grounded his conception (of law) on the ancient principle of the Law of Nature, that he believed in eternal principles of law of which right legislation is merely declaratory'. (P. J. Stanlis, ed. *The Relevance of Edmund Burke* (Washington, 1964), 16–17). Many scholars no longer accept these assumptions. The first suggests a development, an evolution in Burke's thought which is by no means self-evident. The second presupposes that his thought is 'systematic'; as is argued above, this is unlikely when the context of Burke's thought and career have been considered.

Although it is becoming increasingly fashionable to attack the 'new conservatives', there is some danger that in doing so the baby will be thrown out with the bath water and the moral and religious aspects of Burke's philosophy neglected. Nevertheless, scholars have noticed insurmountable objections to the Natural Law interpretation of Burke's thought. First, it is based upon serious misunderstandings of the conception of the Natural Law itself.[4] Second, Burke rarely refers to the Natural Law, suspicious as he was of such abstract ideas. It is strange that a conception which Burke alludes to only on a few occasions should be credited with such significance.[5] Third, Burke's thought was not systematic. It was articulated as a series of responses to a set of political issues. He developed his ideas whenever the occasion required him to do so but at no time did he outline a detailed and systematic political philosophy, still less, one which was not immediately related to public affairs. Those who seek a system in Burke seek in vain.

Commentators who alternatively embark upon a voyage of discovery for some 'key notions' or 'fundamental concepts' fare no better. Burke was frustratingly ambiguous in his discussions of such ideas as contract, divine providence, and, of course, the law of nature. It is equally

---

[4] Its adherents fail to realize the complexity and the subtlety of competing Natural Law traditions within the framework of Medieval Catholicism and early modern Protestantism. Thus, such statements as the following, which attempt to relate Burke's thought to a single Natural Law tradition, need careful qualification. 'The grand Natural Law tradition of Cicero and the Schoolmen, though battered by Hobbes and confused by Locke, re-emerges in all its strength in Burke's reply to the French revolutionaries.' (Russell Kirk's Introduction to P. J. Stanlis, *Edmund Burke and the Natural Law* (Ann Arbor, 1958), vi.) For a fuller discussion of this point than is possible here, see the comments of P. Lucas, 'Edmund Burke's Doctrine of Prescription; or an Appeal from the New to the Old Lawyers', *Historical Journal*, XI (1968), 35–9. It would be interesting to explore the connection between the decline of belief in the Great Chain of Being and the growing rejection in the eighteenth century of the automatic acceptance of a mysterious harmony in the universe and the location of moral duties in the natural order.

[5] Stanlis concedes that Burke's appeals to the Natural Law 'were almost always indirect, through the British constitution, which was for him merely the practical means of guaranteeing the "rights" of Natural Law' (*Edmund Burke and the Natural Law*, 48). The present writer has always found it unusual that Burke rarely refers, either explicitly or even implicitly, to the principles that are supposed to have been the foundations of his thought. Burke was, indeed, uninterested in the workings of the Divine power. 'The instruments which give rise to this mysterious process of nature are not of our making. But out of physical causes unknown to us, perhaps unknowable, arise moral duties which, as we are able perfectly to comprehend, we are bound indispensably to perform.' *The Works of Edmund Burke* (16 vols, 1815–27) VI, 206. (*Appeal from the New to the Old Whigs*, 1791).

unwise to extract a theme or topic from the corpus of his speeches, writings and letters. Such a proceeding fails to relate Burke's thought to the political circumstances which provoked its expression. Burke's thought, indeed, is not as consistent as some of his commentators would like it to be. Morley's famous comment about Burke, that 'He changed his front but he never changed his ground' has been a favourite quotation for too long. Burke *did* change his ground with regard to several important philosophical matters and to obscure the fact does not help us to understand his philosophy. We should emphasize the *absence* of system in Burke's political ideas and underline his characteristic lapses into inconsistency. Only through understanding the flexibility of his thought can we appreciate its richness, its variety and its humanity.

We will not, therefore, attempt to show that Burke was a member of any particular 'school' or 'tradition'. We will not attempt to 'locate' him in the history of political thought. We will not assume that everything which Burke wrote can be treated upon the same level of abstraction. We will not attempt to collect quotations as though they were 'data', from which we may generalize when we have collected a scholarly number. We will not assume that his ideas developed and deepened in a beautiful, logical progression. We will not even assume that Burke's political actions were invariably prompted by political theory. Rather, we will relate his thought to his career and to the political or social situation which evoked it. In doing so, it will be necessary constantly to consider the extent to which the content of Burke's philosophy was affected by the pressures of propaganda. Only through taking these precautions will it be possible to overcome the danger of extracting isolated quotations from Burke and of using them without reference to the attendant circumstances.

The circumstances which provide a framework for considering Burke's political philosophy are those, of course, of his political career. His initial concern was for the welfare of his party, whose history and whose objectives he chose to define in terms of a Whig theory of the British constitution. Then Burke widened his horizons, fastening his attention upon the great imperial problems of America, Ireland and India. Thereafter, he widened his horizons still further, enunciating a theory of politics and of society which he adduced in response to the challenge of the French revolution. We may detect from the most cursory glimpse of Burke's career, therefore, a gathering universality in his concerns. This universality was part of a wider aspect of Burke's thought, one which has not received the consideration which its importance warrants, his originality. Indeed, originality was almost thrust upon Burke for, by the time that he began to write, the language of political thought was no longer suited to the realities of the political situation in Britain.

The Whiggism that Burke inherited from the seventeenth century had become sterile and largely irrelevant to the politics of the reign of George III. John Locke had defended liberty and the ideal of government arising from the consent of the governed within the framework of the laws, for 'where there is no Law, there is no Freedom'.[6] But by 1760 the Whigs had been in power for nearly fifty years. Whiggism had become the ideology of government by the landed aristocracy whose hereditary function it was to mediate between the claims of the prerogative and the rights of the people. Locke had believed, furthermore, that the pursuit of self-interest was a more potent social force than the pursuit of the public interest but he had assumed that the pursuit of individual liberty and the protection of individual rights (to life, liberty and estates) were consistent with the common good. To the Whigs of 1760, however, the connection between the pursuit of the public interest and the pursuit of individual liberty was much weaker than it had been some two generations earlier. In other ways, too, Lockian Whiggism had undergone a transformation of meaning. Locke had equated political power with property. It was left to the Whigs of early Hanoverian England to equate political power with *landed* property. Although, for Locke, the king remained the head of the executive, he remained accountable to the people as represented in parliament. After 1714, however, the realities were very different. The Whigs dominated both houses of parliament and the people's voice could scarcely be heard. In short, Locke's philosophy was much less relevant to the political situation in England in the 1760s than it had been eighty years earlier. In the late seventeenth century Whiggism had been the ideology of opposition, of limited government, of popular rights. In the 1760s it had become the ideology of power.[7] It was to be one of Burke's earliest achievements to cast Whiggism into a fresh mould and to endow it with new purpose and new meaning.

[6] John Locke, *Second Treatise on Government*, P. Laslett, ed. (Cambridge, 1960), 324.

[7] Although this is not the place to plunge into controversial matter, it is worth remarking that if Whiggism had ever acquired a 'possessive' or a proto-capitalistic aspect in the seventeenth century (even though the extent to which MacPherson and others undervalue the strictures placed upon acquisitiveness by writers like Locke is surprising) it had largely lost it during the eighteenth century. That tradition must be sought less in the writings of the English philosophers than in those of Montesquieu, Franklin and the Scottish school.

His Whiggery did not prevent Burke from taking over such ideas and notions as suited him from Bolingbroke and the neo-Harringtonians, the prevalent (and possibly the only) alternative coherent system of political ideas which was current in the second half of the eighteenth century.[8] The classical and humanist ideal of the neo-Harringtonians of the later seventeenth century glorified a polity in which men of property remained independent of the court. They believed that the corruption of the state would result from property becoming dependent upon the government. Bolingbroke thought of politics in terms of property. He regarded the British constitution as a balance of property between the crown and parliament.[9] Through Walpole's 'corrupt' government, and, especially, through his manipulation of royal 'influence', that balance, in Bolingbroke's opinion, was being upset and the constitution endangered. He sought to restore the independence of parliament and to liberate the monarchy from the shackles of oligarchic domination. To this end, Bolingbroke thought it necessary to appeal to the gentry, the traditional governors of the country, men of breeding and manners, and to displace the new monied men whom Walpole was busily attaching to the service of the Whigs. Bolingbroke's attack on Walpole and the Whig system of government was far more than the irate squeals of the 'outs' against the 'ins', more even, than the traditional distinction in British political life between 'court' and 'country'. He was using the language and the concepts of an ideal of society and politics which were quite different in many of their assumptions from the politics of administration and the rule of the aristocracy associated with Walpole and the Whigs. It is not our intention to pursue the subject of Bolingbroke's motivations. It is quite sufficient, for the present, to establish that there existed in the middle of the eighteenth century an ideal and a vocabulary of politics removed from and opposed to that of Walpole and the Whigs.

Burke was a partisan of neither side (of Locke nor of Bolingbroke) but he drew heavily on both of them, fusing elements from each into an ideological synthesis which was purely his own. From Locke he derived his fundamental assumptions about the British constitution,

[8] For a provocative discussion of the neo-Harringtonian tradition in British thought, see J. G. A. Pocock, 'Machiavelli, Harrington and English Political Ideologies in the Eighteenth Century', *William and Mary Quarterly*, XXII (1965).

[9] Recent discussions of Bolingbroke which enlarge upon the notions discussed above include J. Hart, *Viscount Bolingbroke, Tory Humanist* (Toronto, 1965) and I. Kramnick, *The Politics of Nostalgia: Bolingbroke and his Circle* (Harvard, 1968).

from the post-Lockian Whigs his view of a balanced constitution in which an hereditary nobility played a dominant role. But 'influences' in political theory may be double edged; what one thinker takes over from another may be less significant than what he consciously rejects. Burke rejected Locke's idea of contract.[10] He could not derive rights from the contract so he had recourse to a variety of other explanations which, taken together, led Burke to equate rights with obligations, and thus to render his philosophy much less individualistic than that of Locke. Furthermore, although Locke believed that the people had the right to reclaim their sovereignty in certain situations, Burke believed that the location of sovereignty was unalterably settled. In the case of Britain, for example, it was vested in the king and in parliament, an arrangement which no earthly power could alter or amend. From Bolingbroke, on the other hand, Burke derived both the ideal of propertied independence and his horror of corruption. He held that the safety of the constitution was bound up with independence but, unlike Bolingbroke, who had idealized the independence of the gentry, Burke championed the independence of the aristocracy. It was the task of government moreover, to protect property, especially the property of the aristocracy, as a means of minimizing the possibilities of corruption in the state. But whereas Bolingbroke saw the saving of the state in his 'Patriot King' Burke had recourse to an aristocratic party. In this manner, the prevailing concerns of political philosophy guided Burke's thought. He pioneered no novel philosophical method, preferring to remain within the bounds of traditional philosophical discussion, maintaining, yet at the same time, beginning to transform, the old Whiggism.

Edmund Burke was born in Ireland in 1729. He arrived in England in 1750 to continue the legal education he had begun at Trinity College, Dublin. This he soon abandoned in favour of a literary career. His name first came before the public in 1756 when his *Vindication of Natural Society* and the *Sublime and Beautiful* were both published. These were minor, yet distinct, successes and introduced the young Burke into London literary circles. In 1757 he wrote his *Abridgement of English History* (although it was not published until 1812) and, in the same year, co-operated with his kinsman, William Burke, in the composition of the *Account of the European Settlements in America*. In 1758 he began to edit the *Annual Register*, for which he received £100 per annum. But the income from his writings was inadequate

[10] For the reaction against Locke see H. V. S. Ogden, 'The Decline of Lockian Political Theory in England, 1760–1800', *American Historical Review* (1940), 21–44.

to sustain him. He began to seek employment in the more lucrative sphere of politics. After some rebuffs, he obtained the post of private secretary to the Irish Lord Lieutenant's Secretary and he returned to his native land between 1761–4 when he composed his *Tracts on the Popery Laws*. In 1765 he separated from his patron after a bitter dispute concerning his conditions of employment.

Burke had been a writer for about ten years before he became irrevocably committed to politics in 1765. It is tempting to search his early writings for the kernel of what was to come later, but one searches in vain. In fact, no coherent view of politics informs them and most of them are not political works at all. The *Sublime and Beautiful* was a treatise on aesthetics, the *Vindication* a satirical and polemical attack upon the principles of natural philosophy, the *Abridgement* and the *Account* were works of history. Already the extraordinary variety of Burke's interests was apparent but before 1765 he had not committed himself either on politics or political philosophy.

Nobody would seriously deny, however, that the early writings are in some ways a significant anticipation of Burke's political philosophy. Many commentators have noticed, rightly, that the *Vindication* was an attack upon the *a priori* methods of the rationalist philosophers. It was also an attack upon Rousseau's theory of the superiority of natural to civil society. Burke was reluctant to investigate closely the foundations of society for 'the same engines which were employed for the destruction of religion, might be employed with equal success for the subversion of government'.[11] It is important to notice that Burke merely announced his characteristic suspicion of abstract reasoning: he did not as yet choose to apply it to any particular political problem. In much the same way, Burke tentatively approached the large question of the relation of man to religion and Divine Providence. From his student days onwards, Burke had constantly intimated his awareness of a providential order and his understanding of the social functions of religious observances. 'Civil government borrows a strength from ecclesiastical, and artificial laws receive a sanction from artificial revelation.'[12] And although he understood that 'there is nothing of more consequence in a state than the ecclesiastical establishment'[13] he had not yet even begun to consider in any depth either the nature or the extent of religious toleration which a church establishment could safely permit. The reason why he refused to enter into controversy about rights and refrained from discussing the limits of toleration probably arose from the fact that for Burke at this stage of his develop-

[11] *Works*, I, 5 (*Vindication*).   [12] Ibid., 14.
[13] Ibid., X, 380 (*Abridgement*).

ment, these were not human problems at all. Morality was given directly by God.

> Yet we have implanted in us by Providence, ideas, axioms, rules, of what is pious, just, fair, honest, which no political craft, nor learned sophistry, can entirely expel from our breasts.[14]

How far passages such as this provide an early anticipation of Burke's later 'Natural Law' position must briefly be discussed. His *Tracts on the Popery Laws* are usually taken by commentators to support the view that from an early stage of his career Burke appealed to the Natural Law. There is no doubt that Burke referred to it on a number of occasions but a close analysis of his argument diminishes the significance of these references. His attack on the laws discriminating against Catholics in Ireland was directed against the fact that they struck at the foundation of society itself, at the coherence and existence of the family. Nevertheless, such laws did not offend against the 'Natural Law'. They were merely 'unjust, impolitic, and inefficacious against common right and the ends of just government'.[15] Burke took for his standard the view that 'in all forms of government, the people is the true legislature'. A law directed against the majority of the people was thus against the spirit of the law itself. Such a law loses the force of law and becomes void. The law, therefore, provides its own criterion for judging of executive and legislative action; but this criterion does not exist in a vacuum. It arises from a power 'which it is not in the power of any community, or of the whole race of men, to alter'.[16] Because the *will* of God is superior and anterior to the laws of men, human laws are only declaratory because they 'have no power over the substance or original justice'.[17] How far Burke continued to maintain this view during the rest of his career is an interesting question to which we will return later. For the moment, it is enough to suggest that a remark such as this was an acknowledgement of the existence of God and His Law – rather than a recognition of the *relevance* of that law to practical political problems. In fact, Burke's attribution of a principle to the Natural Law is usually a polemical technique which is designed to reinforce the status of the principle itself rather than to illustrate the workings of the Natural Law. In any case, allusions to the Natural Law were not among the most significant characteristics of his writings in this period.

Of considerably greater importance is Burke's recognition of the

---

[14] *Works*, I, 35–6 (*Vindication*).
[16] Ibid., 349.
[15] Ibid., IX, 345 (*Tracts*).
[17] Ibid., 351.

importance of history. His early writings had a powerful historical orientation. Indeed, many of them were in some senses historical projects. In addition to the *Abridgement* and the *Account*, he started a history of the laws of England in the mid-1750s which he abandoned. The *Tracts*, indeed are probably all that Burke managed to complete of a projected history of Ireland. Furthermore, his reviews in the *Annual Register* indicated a fairly sophisticated historical sensibility, not least, a healthy scepticism of fashions of historical writing. Such statements as 'Veneration of antiquity is congenial to the human mind,'[18] might appear to be a foretaste of the later Burke whose political philosophy had such strong historical foundations but there is little justification for such a view. Although Burke's historical debt to Montesquieu was obvious in his ascription of events to environmental causes (in the *Abridgement* and the *Account*) he showed little interest in providing any sort of detailed, empirical analysis. There was scarcely a hint in his early historical works of his concept of prescription and barely an intimation that there might exist a relationship between political theory and history. At the same time, there is nothing to anticipate one of the most important and characteristic aspects of Burke's political philosophy, his idea of the fragility of human societies. Furthermore, his conception of the complexity of social and political units is similarly absent from these works. This is said not to belittle the early works. Taken on their own merits there is much of value in them. But it would be fanciful to imagine that they contained the germ of a 'systematic' or 'developing' philosophy. They contain no such things. They contain, as would have been expected, some few broad hints of the Burke to come but most of the characteristics of his later works are absent from all of these earlier writings, except possibly the *Tracts*.

In much the same way, it is difficult to make out any sort of case for the view that Burke's later political exploits have more than co-incidental origins in these early years. His main, perhaps his only profound, political concern was for the unfashionable country of Ireland. His comments, moreover, on British domestic politics did not display unusual perspicacity. Although his sympathies were at times with the opposition to the court in the early 1760s (in spite of his post in Ireland) his assessments of the political situation in Britain were sometimes amusingly incorrect.[19] There is no trace here

---

[18] *Works*, IX, 370.
[19] Burke to John Ridge, 23 April 1762, *Correspondence*, I, 168–9. These references are to the excellent, modern edition of Burke's *Correspondence*, general editor, T. W. Copeland. The edition is now complete, thus:

of the great career to come, most of which was spent in opposition. On his return to England in 1765 Burke might have been forgiven for bewailing his plight. His literary promise had seemingly not been fulfilled and he had failed in his second career, that of politician. Although he was accepted into London society (he was friendly with the circle of Mrs Montagu) and although he was penetrating the intellectual establishment of the time (he was friendly with David Hume and corresponded with Adam Smith) Burke was no longer a young man. His early career was littered with fragments of works which he had not been able to complete.[20] It was, therefore, only through a series of incredibly lucky chances that Burke's fortunes were saved and the later flowering of philosophical and political talent made possible. In 1765, partly through his connexion with a friendly politician, Charles Townshend, he was offered the post of private secretary to the Marquis of Rockingham. Burke eagerly seized the opportunity, for Rockingham was a rapidly rising politician and became Prime Minister in July 1765. Burke was at once drawn into the centre of the political world. In the December of Burke's *annus mirabilis*, a friend of Rockingham, Lord Verney, brought him into parliament for the rotten borough of Wendover. It was not long before Burke made an impact on the Commons through his command of fact and the power of his oratory. When the Rockingham ministry fell in July 1766 Burke went into opposition with his master, in spite of offers from the new ministers.

It was not, however, until November 1766 that Burke can be said *finally* to have decided to remain with Rockingham in opposition. (There is some evidence to suggest that he may have been willing to serve with the new ministry.)[21] His rejection of the ministerial overtures

Vol. I to 1768, T. W. Copeland, ed. (1958).
Vol. II, 1768–74, L. S. Sutherland, ed. (1960).
Vol. III, 1774–8, G. H. Guttridge, ed. (1961).
Vol. IV, 1778–82, J. A. Woods, ed. (1963).
Vol. V, 1782–9, H. Furber, ed. (1965).
Vol. VI, 1789–91, A. Cobban and R. A. Smith, eds. (1967).
Vol. VII, 1792–4, P. J. Marshall and J. A. Woods, eds. (1968).
Vol. VIII, 1794–6, R. B. McDowell, ed. (1969).
Vol. IX, 1796–7, R. B. McDowell and J. A. Woods, eds. (1970).

[20] In addition to the works already mentioned, there survives a fragment of *Hints for an Essay on the Drama.*

[21] There is strong evidence to support the view that Burke's connection with the Rockinghams was by no means as close or as complete as the Whig historians of the nineteenth century liked to believe. After the fall of the Rockingham Ministry in July 1766 Burke did *not* irrevocably commit himself to the Whig leader (Burke to Charles O'Hara, 10 August 1766, *Correspondence,*

of November 1766 confirmed Burke in his new and unexpected role, that of party politician, and servant of the Marquis of Rockingham.

I, 264). It was Burke himself who began, a few years later, to put a story around that there had never been any question of his deserting the Rockingham Whigs. (Burke to Dr William Markham, *post*-November 1771, ibid., II, 269–70).

Chapter I

The Philosopher of Party

Edmund Burke had decided his political allegiance but his commitment to the Rockingham Whigs did not carry with it the slightest assurance that he would enjoy predominant influence among them. Indeed, for two hundred years his role in the Rockingham Whig party has been greatly exaggerated; in spite of his great talents and his enormous industry, Burke remained the servant – he did not become the master – of the Whig Lords. He was never considered for a cabinet office and did not believe that his pretensions were sufficient to warrant one. He well understood that the highest offices in the state were not for the likes of an Irish adventurer. In the same way, although Burke was the greatest orator of this period his talents never won him the leadership of his party in the House of Commons. Until his death in 1774, William Dowdeswell, a reliable but dull Worcestershire squire, led the Rockingham party in the lower house, to be succeeded for two years by the charming yet hopelessly inefficient Lord John Cavendish.[1] After 1776 Charles James Fox dominated his party in the Commons.[2] Furthermore, Burke was too personally dependent upon Rockingham ever to think of establishing an independent political career for himself. It was not just that Burke believed that the business of building up an electoral interest based upon landed property was not for men like him. Like other members of his family Edmund was something of a failure as a man of business and he remained of necessity dependent

[1] One of the best loved and least competent members of the Rockingham Whig establishment. He represented various constituencies between 1754 and 1790.
[2] The darling of the radicals and a man whose personal attraction was as compelling for contemporaries as it is inexplicable to historians. Charles Fox began his political career as a ministerialist but gave up his office as a Lord of the Admiralty in 1772. Thereafter he drifted into opposition to North's ministry, made a name for himself by his opposition to the war against America and became a national figure during the Petitioning Movement of 1779–80.

upon the Marquis of Rockingham. Burke was a follower not a leader. He never resented his exclusion from the aristocratic centre of the party for it was never his ambition to find a place for himself within it.

In 1765, however, Burke appears to have thrown himself into his new situation with characteristic force and vigour. The Duke of Newcastle, one of the party grandees, complained that 'Burke was so constantly going to and fro that I could scarcely collect his opinion'.[3] And although he was not responsible for any of the major decisions of the first Rockingham ministry (July 1765–July 1766) he defended its policies with great skill in the Commons. He began to revel in the tumultuous world of politics and began to cut something of a figure upon the public stage. His defence of the ministry's American policy – repeal of the Stamp Act but the passing of a Declaratory Act reserving the constitutional right of the British parliament to impose internal taxation upon the colonists – won him immediate recognition albeit of a modest character. Edmund Burke had arrived in politics; he had won his spurs in parliament and he had won a place for himself in his party.

After 1766 there occurred little alteration in Burke's position in the Rockingham Whig party. The limited nature of his influence was evident during the next few years. In the session of 1767, for example, Burke played little part in the formulation of the Rockinghams' policy towards the East India Company, the greatest issue of the session, and he remained indifferent to his party's factious support of a scheme to reduce the land tax from 4s to 3s in the £. In 1768 he played a similarly passive role both in parliament and at the general election of that year. Most significant of all, in the PETITIONING MOVEMENT of 1769, although he played a considerable role in moving Rockingham to activity, he exerted in fact, little real influence over the tactics adopted by his party in its involvement with this first phase of English radicalism. It was Dowdeswell, not Burke, who was the architect of the party's policy of cautious support for the petitions. As for the counties, it required the endeavours of the Whig Lords in mobilizing their tenants to make a reality of the radical movement. Burke's importance in his party can easily be exaggerated. He never desired a position of over-whelming influence. Even if he had, his Whig masters would never have allowed him to attain it. As Burke himself put it: 'I am no leader my Lord, not do I ever answer for the Conduct of anyone but myself'.[4]

---

[3] M. Bateson (ed.), *The Duke of Newcastle's Narrative of Changes in the Ministry, 1765–7* (1898), 121.

[4] Burke to Dr William Markham, *post*-9 November 1771, *Correspondence*, II, 269–70.

Nevertheless, from the earliest days of his attachment to the Rocking-ham Whig party Burke, as a writer, had been entrusted by Rockingham with the task of justifying the activities of his party. As early as 1766 he had written *A Short Account of a Late Short Administration*, a defence of the record of the first Rockingham ministry. The pamphlet was unremarkable and succeeded in anticipating nothing of Burke's later party theory. (The pamphlet did not even mention the word 'party'.) He was defending the record of a particular ministry not a general concept of government. Thus he recounted the achievements of the ministry in glowing terms but he failed to explain how such a successful ministry, enjoying the support of public opinion, failed to maintain itself in office. As a partisan of the Rockinghams, Burke discreetly drew a veil over the chronic interval divisions which wracked the ministry. Although he ascribed all the difficulties faced by the ministers to the opposition of certain placemen[5] he completely failed to invest this phenomenon with the significance which he was later to assign to other manifestations of court intrigue. The absence of even the glimmerings of a party ideology not only in this early tract but also in the other writings and speeches of this period strongly suggests not only that Burke did *not* come to the Rockingham party with a theory of party to impose upon it but also that he did not embrace such a theory of party at all at this stage. Yet in 1769 and again in 1770 Burke proceeded to enunciate his theory of party in some detail. The question naturally arises, therefore, of where Burke derived his idea of party.

The answer is quite simple; Burke derived it from the experiences of the Rockingham Whigs themselves. He had not long been among them when he began to imbibe the myths and the prejudices of the party, the strongest of which was the myth of the influence of Lord Bute.[6] It was to the king's *quondam* favourite that the Rockinghams ascribed the cause of all their difficulties and, in particular, the res-ponsibility for the apparent anti-aristocratic policy of the reign of George III, a policy which was manifested in the Massacre of the

[5] Several of whom had held office under George Grenville (1763–5) and thus acquired responsibility for his American policy. When the Rockingham ministry (1765–6) proceeded to reverse his policies, they naturally voted against it. Burke and others incorrectly ascribed their behaviour to the insidious plotting of the court.

[6] The king's tutor whom George III brought into politics in March 1761. He remained by his side until his retirement in April 1763. His close and affectionate relationship with the young king and the inability of the older Whigs to displace him in the king's estimation aroused considerable envy among them.

Pelhamite Innocents[7] and in the fall of the first Rockingham ministry. Of course, they exaggerated Bute's importance – which rapidly declined after April 1763 – but the 'Bute Myth' raised important constitutional questions, such as the extent of the royal prerogative of appointing ministers, the relation between the crown and its ministers, the relation between the ministers and the legislature. It opened a chasm of mistrust between the Rockinghams and George III and contributed largely to their reluctance to take office after 1766. Burke's doctrine of party was a Rockinghamite riposte to Lord Bute: government by party would render government by favourite impossible. In this, as in so much else, Burke was echoing Rockingham's sentiments, not prompting them. In a very real sense, Edmund Burke was his master's voice.

The 'Bute Myth' was not the only Rockinghamite justification for the party's exclusion from power after 1766. The finger of blame also pointed at Lord Chatham, upon whose lack of co-operation Rockingham had partly blamed the downfall of the Rockingham ministry in the summer of 1766. It was towards the end of that year that Burke began to echo the party's catch-phrases about the Great Commoner who had come to power amidst the ruins of the Rockingham ministry. 'Lord Bute, to be sure, is uncertain and unquiet in his Nature; but who *will* do more, who *can* do more, to satisfy him, than the present Minister.'[8] Burke had entered upon the political scene somewhat too late to share to the full his party's hatred of Bute but he was just in time to experience the bitterness which they felt towards Chatham, a man who had suffered the same proscription as themselves at the hands of Bute but who had evidently proceeded to throw in his lot with the court.

In seeking to defend his party against Bute and Chatham, Burke sought to relate the principles of his party to those of traditional Whiggism. As he wrote in 1791 in the *Appeal from the New to the Old Whigs*, 'When he entered into the Whig party, he did not conceive that they pretended to any discoveries.' For Burke it was the duty of good Whigs in the 1760s to preserve the constitution, to maintain the Hanoverian succession and, in their natural function as leaders of society, to govern the country by counselling the king. The king and Bute were guilty of

[7] The dismissal from offices (both in local and central government) of those who voted against the Bute ministry in December 1762 on the issue of peace with France and Spain. On an issue of confidence such as this, it was only reasonable that the court would discipline those office-holders who refused to support the king's administration. The victims of the Massacre, however, were, not unnaturally, disposed to ascribe their martyrdom to the sinister plans of Lord Bute, the king's favourite.

[8] Burke to Charles O'Hara, 23 December 1766, *Correspondence*, I, 284–5.

dangerous innovation in ridding the public service of those who were the traditional rulers of the country. Such sentiments chimed in well with the unspoken assumptions of the aristocratic Rockingham Whig leaders. Burke's application of the Whig tradition to the Rockingham Whigs was beautifully tailored to suit the instinctive cliquishness and the co-operative spirit of the lords of the Rockingham party.

In 1769 and in 1770 Burke published pamphlets which set out his general theory of party. In the former year, his *Observations on a Late Pamphlet Intituled a State of the Nation* was published anonymously followed in April 1770 by his more famous *Thoughts on the Cause of the Present Discontents*. There can be little doubt that suspicion of Chatham was the most powerful single motivation in Burke's mind during his composition of the *Thoughts*. While he was busy putting his party thoughts down on paper, the PETITIONING MOVEMENT of 1769 was proceeding apace, to culminate, the Rockinghams hoped and expected, in the fall of the Grafton ministry[9] and its replacement by a ministry which included both Chatham and Rockingham. Yet who was to lead it? It was to the debate provoked by this question that Burke contributed his party writings. He tried to demonstrate that the Rockinghams had claims to leadership which were superior to those of Chatham. This he strove to do in a subtle and delicate manner, lest Chatham be so offended that he damage the fragile unity of the opposition. This is why Burke attacked the principles rather than the personality of Chatham. In attempting to establish the claims of the Rockinghams to lead the opposition in the peculiar conditions of 1769, therefore, Burke went so far as to *justify* the constitutional principles of the Rockinghams (not to invent them) over and against those of Chatham.[10] To inform himself on party affairs he looked over the party's papers and letters of the last few years to show, as he confided to Rockingham, how 'past experience had informed us of nothing but

[9] The Grafton ministry replaced that of Chatham in 1768. Its unhappy history was marred by the Middlesex election affair of 1768 when the ministry, through its parliamentary majority, attempted to exclude John Wilkes from the parliamentary seat to which he was thrice elected. The Rockingham Whigs, in uneasy alliance with Chatham, Grenville and the metropolitan radicals took the issue to the country. Petitions demanding the dissolution of parliament were raised in a score of towns and counties.

[10] Burke was striving to present to the public the Rockinghams' solution to the 'Discontents' of the age as well as claiming the leadership of the opposition for his master. For an interpretation which concentrates upon the latter almost to the exclusion of the former, see J. Brewer, 'Party and the Double Cabinet: Two Facets of Burke's "Thoughts"', *Historical Journal*, vol. XIV (1971), 484–6.

his Enmity to your whole system of men and Opinions'.[11] Indeed, Chatham's principles were fundamentally different from those of the Rockinghams. He found planned combination in politics an anathema; he wished to maintain his independence and freedom of action until he was summoned by the king to form a ministry, when he would demand the full exercise of the royal prerogative of appointing ministers. Neither Burke nor Rockingham could find any room for compromise with such opinions. Burke's party theory is an explanation and a justification of their refusal to compromise.

Burke had at least one further motive in publicizing his party ideas: he hoped that their impact upon the Rockingham party would strengthen its cohesion. His theory of party was just as much an *apologia* for the Rockingham Whigs as a defence of any *system* of government. This, at least was what Rockingham hoped it would be. He hoped that Burke's ideas would equally justify the present opinions of his friends as much as their past conduct.[12] It was, indeed, at Rockingham's instigation that the *Thoughts* were written at all. 'I think it would take universally, and tend to form and to unite a party upon real and well founded principles', he wrote.[13] Burke thought that he was successful in this. 'It is the political creed of our party', he proclaimed.[14] Yet the party would be nothing without the support of public opinion. 'The public in general have never as yet had a fair State of our Principles laid before them – In my opinion they will like them.'[15] He persuaded himself that they did. In May 1770 he affirmed that the *Thoughts* had won 'the approbation of the most thinking part of the people'.[16] The theory of party, for Burke, had fulfilled its immediate political objectives.

The starting point for Burke's party thought was his conviction that the country was afflicted with the evil consequence of the court's attack upon the aristocracy and the traditional constitution. These 'Present Discontents' could be cured only through the agency of party. Burke began to describe them in the *Observations* when he referred to the plans of the court 'long pursued, with but too fatal a success . . . to break the strength of this kingdom by frittering down the bodies which compose it, by fomenting bitter and sanguinary animosities, and by dissolving every tie of social affection and public trust'.[17] The

[11] Burke to Rockingham, October 1769, *Correspondence*, II, 88.
[12] Rockingham to Burke, 4 November 1769, ibid., 104.
[13] Rockingham to Burke, 15 October 1769, ibid., 92.
[14] Burke to Richard Shackleton, 6 May 1770, ibid., 150.
[15] Burke to Rockingham, *post*-6 November 1769, ibid., 108–9.
[16] Burke to Richard Shackleton, 6 May 1770, loc. cit.
[17] *Works*, II, 11.

malaise of social and political dissensions had in Britain traditionally been associated in the public mind with party conflict but, as Burke wrote in an important passage in the *Thoughts*: 'the great parties which formerly divided and agitated the kingdom are known to be in a manner entirely dissolved'.[18] It was all the more curious then,

> That Government is at once dreaded and contemned; that the laws are despoiled of all their respected and salutory terrors; that their inaction is a subject of ridicule, and their exertion of abhorrence; that rank, and office, and title, and all the solemn plausibilities of the world have lost their reverence and effect . . . that hardly anything above or below, abroad or at home, is sound and entire; but that disconnexion and confusion, in offices, in parties, in families, in Parliament, in the nation, prevail beyond the disorders of any former time.[19]

Burke did not ascribe the political and social instability of the time to the court itself but to the cant of blind and indiscriminate support of government, 'He that supports every Administration, subverts all Government.' Such a man does nothing to strengthen government because he is 'open to continual shocks and changes, upon the principles of the meanest cabal, and the most contemptible intrigue'.[20] Burke denied the court maxim, 'That all political connexions are in their nature factious, and as such ought to be dissipated and destroyed.'[21] He was confident that there existed a large number of honest men who could resist the blandishments of the court and who, through the agency of party, would be willing to play their part in contesting the establishment in Britain of a sinister royal absolutism.

Burke feared not only the principles of the court but also the means by which it sought to translate its loyalist ideals into practical politics. The great object of the court cabal was 'to secure to the Court the un-limited and uncontrouled use of its own vast influence, under the sole direction of its own private favour'.[22] To this end, the court wished to establish a 'double cabinet', a second administration, which would be both separate from, and more powerful than, the responsible ministry, enjoying, as it would, the extensive range of royal influence as a source of bribery and corruption. Through these means, the court cabal would build up for itself a party of 'King's Friends' who would render parliament acquiescent in the whole scheme. Burke believed that the destruction of the constitution presaged the breakdown of government and a military coup. The victory of the court would not

[18] *Works*, II, 220 (*Thoughts*). [19] Ibid., 220. [20] Ibid., 326.
[21] Ibid., 329. [22] Ibid., 231.

result in firm government for the court system, according to Burke, 'not only strikes a palsy into every nerve of our free constitution, but in the same degree benumbs and stupifies the whole executive power: rendering Government in all its grand operations languid, uncertain, ineffective'.[23] The acquiescence of the governed might ultimately have to be effected through force of arms. The court system, for Burke, was thus symptomatic of a new and sinister threat to the liberties and constitution of Great Britain.

How much credence can be given to Burke's analysis of the 'Present Discontents'? He was, of course, perfectly justified in calling attention to the unusual nature of the politics of the 1760s, the instability of ministries, the weakness and unpopularity of government, the fragmentation of connections and, most important of all, the demise of the great parties. None of these, however, had their origin in court plots. Indeed, historians no longer believe in the myth of the 'King's Friends' nor take seriously the idea of a court cabal. There never was a conscious attempt by the court, even in the days of Lord Bute, to undermine the role of parliament in the constitution or to make ministries dependent upon the court. Furthermore, although there can be little doubt that the king and the court disliked party combinations and that they were reluctant to have them in office upon a party basis, there is nothing to substantiate Burke's claim that the court had embarked upon a deliberate policy of taking the powers of government out of the hands of ministers and placing them into those of creatures of its own selection. Even if they had intended to do so, it is very doubtful indeed if George III and Lord Bute had the ability to envisage, let alone to execute, the kind of far-reaching scheme which Burke imputed to them. In long-term political planning they were woefully deficient. They had neither the political skill nor the personal nerve seriously to undertake a constitutional revolution.

Why did Burke indulge in this kind of misrepresentation? To a considerable extent he was merely echoing some of the traditional 'country' prejudices of the century. A generation earlier Bolingbroke had raised his standard in opposition to the luxury and the wealth which gave rise to the corruption which, he alleged, maintained his arch-enemy, Walpole, in office. It is important to recognize that such conceptions were an integral and essential part of the political language of the age. The influence of Machiavelli, or, at least, the eighteenth-century version of Machiavelli, was such as to rivet public attention to the morality of the leading men of the age, whose corruption led to national degeneracy and whose virtue led to national well-being. The

[23] *Works*, II, 271 (*Thoughts*).

eighteenth-century mind was concerned less with the morality of individuals than with the corruption of individuals as a symptom of a deeper malaise: the corruption of the state through the unbalancing of the delicate system of checks and balances which maintained the mixed constitution. Burke was saturated in this kind of thinking. He believed that the sinister operations of the court cabal and the engine of royal influence were spreading corruption like an infectious disease through the state. Bolingbroke had looked to his 'Patriot King' to effect the restoration of virtue. Edmund Burke called upon the principles of party to do the same. In so doing he was following a popular contemporary belief that a state which had 'fallen' could only be reformed or restored if it returned to the principles upon which it had been founded. Almost inevitably, therefore, Burke's solution of the problem of the 'Present Discontents' involved a reassertion of traditional principles, in this case those of the Whigs of the period of the Glorious Revolution.

Burke was, therefore, perhaps more inclined to define what a party ought to *be* rather than to explain what a party ought to *do*. It is no accident that the best known aspect of his party theory is his *definition* of party: 'a body of man united for prompting by their joint endeavours the national interest, upon some particular principle in which they are all agreed'.[24] In defending the principledness of party Burke was careful to protect himself from the charge that a strict adherence to party dogma violated that independence of judgement which the eighteenth century valued so highly:

> as the greater part of the measures which arise in the course of public business are related to or dependent on some great *leading general principles in Government*, a man must be peculiarly unfortunate in the choice of his political company if he does not agree with them at least nine times in ten.[25]

The function of party men was not to nurse their untainted virtue in opposition but, by every constitutional and legal means, to seek power. A party ministry need not absolutely exclude non-party men but the large majority of places would go to party men. But, the most important offices must not go to men 'who contradict the very fundamental principles upon which every fair connexion must stand'.[26] Party enabled honest men to achieve a reassertion of the fundamental principles of the constitution. The 'Present Discontents' would disappear once there came into office a ministry dependent for its existence not upon the whim of a favourite but upon the support of a majority in the

[24] *Works*, II, 335.   [25] Ibid., 339.   [26] Ibid., 336.

House of Commons, for not only the strength and energy but also the representative nature of the British constitution would be re-established.

Two aspects of Burke's doctrine of party have been much misunderstood by commentators, the question of the ubiquity of party and the question of the permanence of party. On one level, Burke argued that in any state parties were essential to the preservation of freedom. He refuted the view that they were vicious aberrations from normal political life. 'Party divisions, whether on the whole operating for good or evil, are things inseparable from free government.'[27] They 'have always existed and they always will'.[28] The ubiquity of parties in free states did not logically entail, however, that parties should be a *permanent* part of every free constitution. As he wrote in the *Thoughts*: 'It is not every conjuncture which calls with equal force upon the activity of honest men; but critical exigencies now and then arise, and I am mistaken if this be not one of them.'[29] Party was, therefore, an ever-present political practice to which recourse might be had in exceptional circumstances.[30] There is no need to assume that Burke believed that party should be permanent.

Indeed, we should avoid the temptation to jump to the conclusion that Burke thought in terms of a party *system*. He conceived of party as a temporary expedient, a means of resolving problems within a static political system. He did not think of party in the context of a developing constitution. He did not think of party as a dynamic force, affecting the development of the British constitution. If the British political system were in need of reform, then reforming endeavours must be directed towards restoring the constitution to its original principles not towards changing the nature of the constitution itself. Party was, therefore, a profoundly conservative force. The idea that the British political system might move towards a two party system of government was entirely absent from Burke's mind. The *restoration* of the constitution which Burke envisaged was to be achieved not through the institutionalization of party conflict but by bringing

[27] *Works*, II, 9 (*Observations*).

[28] Burke to Richard Shackleton, 25 May 1779, *Correspondence*, IV, 79.

[29] *Works*, II, 341 (*Thoughts*).

[30] This interpretation of Burke's idea of party differs slightly from that of Dr Brewer (*supra n.* 10) who comments that because none of Burke's colleagues in the Rockingham party expressed surprise at Burke's references to party in the *Thoughts* then Burke was less interested in pioneering a novel concept of party than in claiming the leadership of the opposition for the Rockinghams. Burke's idea of party, of course, was *not* a novel concept and there was, therefore, no reason for his colleagues to express surprise at it.

virtuous men into government through the agency of party, and thus by ending, not prolonging, the political partisanship of the reign of George III. Party was Burke's vehicle for annihilating conflict and, as such, was not capable of political change or constitutional development, in his political theory.

These considerations help to explain what is otherwise inexplicable – Burke's neglect of the organizational side of party. He never seriously entertained the prospect that a party ought to seek to augment its numbers in the lower house, preferring to rely, with astonishing sanguinity, upon the good-will of other groups. In an intellectual and political climate which accepted the assumption that political power stemmed from property and not from people – an assumption which Burke keenly defended – it was impossible for him to conceive of a ministerial party, independent of the king, resting upon a parliamentary majority, representing the body of the nation. Burke thus appears to reject the concepts and developments which later generations have come to associate with party government. In fact, he became unhappy when, in the 1790s, politics acquired a superficial polarity during the contest between Pitt and Fox 'and that there appears a sort of necessity of adopting the one or the other of them, without regard to any public principle whatsoever. This extinguishes party as party'.[31] It is, therefore, extremely doubtful if Professor Cone's assessment can be accepted: that Burke in 1770 'already perceived the lines which England's political and constitutional development would follow'.[32] It does Burke's reputation no good both to claim too much for his perspicacity and also to attribute to him ideas which he explicitly rejected.

Edmund Burke's traditional title to the role of prophet of the two party system is thus unacceptable – and not only because he did not believe in a party system. He may have been the greatest but he was certainly not the first propagandist of party. Since the later seventeenth century the isolated individuals who defended the principle of party had become a steady trickle. The early stalwarts of party thought in terms of a state divided by *religious* parties, a state in which toleration could only be established by one church 'balancing' another. Gradually, however, as parties developed in England, especially after 1688–9, so an initial reluctance to admit their legitimacy gradually lapsed into a critical acceptance of their constitutional functions. The ambivalent attitude of the eighteenth century towards political parties was reflected in the fact that the Walpolean Whigs who condemned opposition

[31] Burke to Lord Fitzwilliam, 2 September 1796, *Correspondence*, IX, 77–80.
[32] Carl B. Cone, *Burke and the Nature of Politics: The Age of the American Revolution* (University of Kentucky Press, 1957), 203.

33

parties regarded party organizations among their own number in a favourable light[33] and even that great scourge of party, Bolingbroke, not only admitted the legitimacy of opposition but also acknowledged the permissibility of a 'national' party.[34] Already, in Bolingbroke, exists the distinction between opposition to the throne and opposition to the crown's ministers.[35] The only possible conclusion, therefore, is that not only the principles of the Rockingham Whigs but also the conception of party itself had become political commonplaces even before Burke.

The novelty of Burke's idea of party consists less in its content than in the circumstances of its exposition. The fact that Burke was applying to the political problems of his day a traditional nostrum does not render his theory of party spurious. There can be no doubt that Burke was completely sincere in what he wrote although his work represented an accurate, if highly elaborate synthesis of Rockinghamite principles, myths, grudges and prejudices. Similarly, there can be no doubt that the political philosophy which he fashioned from these unpromising materials was advanced in no self-interested manner. For Burke's enunciation of the theory of party damaged the relations of his party with Chatham and with the radicals.

As we have seen, the *Thoughts* was nothing less than a public rejection of Chathamite political principles. He attacked the Chathamite maxim, 'Not Men but Measures' as 'a sort of charm, by which many people get loose from every honourable engagement'.[36] He admitted that 'power arising from popularity', the Chathamite principle, was just as much a security for the rights of the people as the Rockinghamite maxim of 'power arising from connexion'. The weakness of Chathamite principles was that they depended entirely upon the personal, and therefore, transient, power and reputation of one man. Those of the Rockinghams were rooted in the country.[37] This did not mean that Burke neglected the importance of personality in politics. On the contrary, his conception of party embraced a profound appreciation of its significance: 'Constitute Government how you please, infinitely the greater part of it must depend upon the exercise of the powers which are left at large to the prudence and uprightness of Ministers of State. Even all the use and potency of the laws depends upon them'.[38] And he went on to insist:

Before men are put forward into the great trusts of the State, they

[33] I. Kramnick, *The Politics of Nostalgia: Bolingbroke and his Circle* (Harvard, 1968), 121–4.
[34] Ibid., 59.   [35] Ibid., 153–63, *passim*.
[36] *Works*, II, 337 (*Thoughts*).   [37] Ibid., 239.   [38] Ibid., 260.

ought by their conduct to have obtained such a degree of estimation in their country, as may be some sort of pledge and security to the public, that they will not abuse those trusts. It is no mean security for proper use of power, that a man has shown by the general tenor of his actions, that the affection, the good opinion, the confidence, of his fellow citizens have been among the principle objects of his life; and that he has owed none of the gradations of power or fortune to a settled contempt, or occasional forfeiture of their esteem.[39]

Burke, of course, argued that this security is best obtained in party combination. How, he asked, could a man sit for years in parliament 'without seeing any one sort of men, whose character, conduct, or disposition, would lead him to associate himself with them, to aid and be aided, in any one system of public utility'?[40] The function of party, therefore was, 'To bring the dispositions that are lovely in private life into the service and conduct of the commonwealth; so to be patriots, as not to forget we are gentlemen.'[41]

It was therefore, not merely political institutions that needed changing. Indeed, the institutions ought not to be tampered with. It was the *men* who needed to be changed. Party was the vehicle by which this change would be effected:

Whilst men are linked together, they easily and speedily communicate the alarm of an evil design. They are enabled to fathom it with common counsel, and to oppose it with united strength. Whereas, when they lie dispersed, without concert, order, or discipline, communication is undertaken counsel difficult, and resistance impracticable. . . .

In a connexion, the most inconsiderable man, by adding to the weight of the whole, has his value, and his use; out of it, the greatest talents are wholly unserviceable to the public.[42]

The virtuous men of the Rockingham party, then, were Burke's answer to the political corruption and moral degeneracy of the age.

Burke never wearied of underlining how acting in corps strengthened a man's principles and stiffened him sufficiently to resist the temptations of court emoluments. Party was made for man's weakness for without it he was too weak and vulnerable to maintain correct political principles in the world. Party enabled him to develop his political and moral capacities to the full.[43] Burke's idea of party, therefore, conformed to his view of human nature. Of parties, he noted in 1779,

[39] *Works*, II, 264–5 (*Thoughts*).   [40] Ibid., 340.   [41] Ibid., 340–1.
[42] Ibid., 329–30.   [43] Ibid., 328–32.

I have observed but three sorts of men that have kept out of them. Those who profess nothing but a pursuit of their own interests, and who avow their resolution of attaching themselves to the present possession of power, in whose ever hands it is, or however it may be used. The other sort are ambitious men, of light or no principles, who in their turns make use of all parties, and therefore avoid entering into what may be construed an engagement with any. The other sort is hardly worth mentioning, being composed only of four or five Country Gentlemen of little efficiency in public business.[44]

Burke derived his theory from no abstract source and he sought for no external criterion of behaviour outside the nature of man himself. This is hardly surprising since the 'Present Discontents' were at bottom, a breakdown in man's public responsibility and a lapse of his moral control. Party will remedy these failings because it is rooted in man and designed to further the standards of his public activities.

Burke's reluctance to embrace the increasingly popular radical ideas for curing the 'Present Discontents' may now become clear. We should remember that the temptation for Burke to have included in his political manifesto some of the radical demands must have been very strong. During the Petitioning Movement of 1769 the Rockinghams had attempted to work with the radicals in the country. If they had embraced some part of the radical programme then they would have received that enthusiastic, popular following of which the aristocratic Rockingham Whigs always stood badly in need. Yet there was far more to Burke's rejection of radicalism than his reflection of the aristocratic prejudices of the Rockingham party. Fundamentally, he did not believe that the various planks in the radical programme would do anything to reduce the 'Present Discontents'. More frequent elections, for example, would simply allow the court a more frequent opportunity of corrupting electors. This prospect deeply alarmed Burke for he believed that any extension of court influence would only serve to undermine the power of the landed interest.[45] He was prepared to take place bills much more seriously. Nevertheless, the desire to enhance the right of free election clashed with another constitutional maxim, the principle of the mixture of powers in the constitution. Burke was not opposed in principle to a ministry having some influence with the lower house so long as the influence in question was open and visible. He would have retained the system by which

[44] Burke to Richard Shackleton, 25 May 1779, loc. cit.
[45] For Burke believed that the country gentlemen would be no match for the court interest in prolonged and violent electoral struggles. *Works*, II, 319–20 (*Thoughts*).

ministers and office-holders retained their relationship with the legislature.[46] Burke was haunted by the curious fear that the mixed constitution revered by the Whig theorists, would give way to a legislature completely independent of (and in danger of confrontation with) the executive. As for the radical demand for the widening of the franchise, Burke could not see how increasing the numbers could lead to a freer parliament. Burke, in fact, would have *reduced* rather than increased the size of the electorate.[47] No wonder that the radicals of the metropolis, having recently rediscovered their intellectual heritage of the seventeenth century, reacted strongly when Burke's mordant logic threatened to make nonsense of their principles. No wonder that one of the most immediate, yet longest lasting, consequences of Burke's publication of his party ideas was the weakening of the relationship between the Rockinghams and the radicals. Burke's redefinition of Whiggism, therefore, patently left no room within it for radical ideology.

So far we have considered only those aspects of Burke's theory of party which were rooted in the political circumstance of the Rockingham Whigs in the decade of the 1760s. There remain to be discussed certain general themes within it which cannot immediately be related to political matters. Among these must be included Burke's peculiar conception of history. This appears to have operated at more than one level. For example, he acknowledged his indebtedness to the common law school of the seventeenth century. Its adherents believed in the ancient constitution of Anglo-Saxon times, whose freedom from corruption and whose popular basis contrasted strongly with the sterile and corrupt political system of Hanoverian England.[48] It is by no means clear that the reader ought to accept naively Burke's belief in the Anglo-Saxon constitution. It is not clear how seriously Burke took it himself.

Many a stern republican, after gorging himself with a full feast of admiration of the Grecian commonwealths and of our true Saxon constitution, and disgorging all the splendid bile of his virtuous indignation on King John and King James, sits down perfectly satisfied to the coarsest and homeliest job of the day he lives in.[49]

[46] *Works*, II, 321-3 (*Thoughts*).

[47] Ibid., VIII, 140-1 (*First Letter on a Regicide Peace*).

[48] These ideas had been perpetuated and popularized in eighteenth-century England by none other than Bolingbroke. See I. Kramnick, op. cit., 177-81. For the seventeenth-century origins of the common law school see the classic statement by J. G. A. Pocock, *The Ancient Constitution and the Feudal Law* (Cambridge University Press, 1957), especially chapters two, three and four.

[49] *Works*, II, 226-7 (*Thoughts*).

More seriously, Burke ransacked history for examples which would support his arguments. He affirmed that in ancient times parties were well known and much respected.[50] More recently, during the reign of Anne, parties had been an integral part of the British political system.[51] The reason for this lay deep in the fabric of the constitution after the Glorious Revolution. In a crucial passage in the *Thoughts* Burke describes how after the Glorious Revolution, the monarchy was too weak to manage a distracted kingdom:

> The Court was obliged therefore to delegate a part of its powers to men of such interest as could support, and of such fidelity as would adhere to, its establishment. Such men were to draw in a greater number to a concurrence in the common defence. This connexion, necessary at first, continued long after convenient; and properly conducted might indeed in all situations, be a useful instrument of Government. At the same time, through the intervention of men of popular weight and character, the people possessed a security for their just proportion of importance in the State. But as the title to the Crown grew stronger by long possession, and by the constant increase of its influence, these helps have of late seemed to certain persons no better than incumbrances.[52]

Historic precedent, constitutional necessity and political practice, therefore, vindicated party government. Although Burke could not claim that the court system violated 'the letters of any law', he was confident that it offended against the *spirit* of the constitution established at the Glorious Revolution.

It also offended against Burke's elitist concept of aristocratic government.[53] He was naturally concerned to defend the Whig aristocracy, especially after the misfortunes they had suffered at the hands of George III, but his justification of Whig aristocratic power was far more complex and far more subtle than political convenience alone required. For Burke it was both natural and desirable that government would reside in the hands of the aristocracy. 'While they are men of property, it is impossible to prevent it.'[54] Burke accepted the assumption of his age that political power should correspond to property and not to opinion. Yet for him the political power of the aristocracy was not merely a crude manifestation of its propertied power. Its influence should rest upon the favour of the people, who should 'never be duped into an opinion, that such greatness in a Peer is the despotism of an

[50] *Works*, II, 332–3.   [51] Ibid., 334.   [52] Ibid., 230.
[53] Burke to William Weddell, 31 January 1792, *Correspondence*, VII, 50–63.
[54] *Works*, II, 245 (*Thoughts*).

aristocracy, when they know and feel it to be the effect and pledge of their own importance'.[55] Nevertheless, Burke was aware of a host of good reasons why the aristocracy enjoyed a natural right to govern.

> Long possession of Government; vast property; obligations of favours given and received; connexion of office; ties of blood, of alliance, of friendship . . . the name of Whig, dear to the majority of the people; the zeal early begun and steadily continued to the Royal Family.[56]

Party for Burke was a means of placing at the disposal of the state these attributes of the aristocracy. Late in his life he reflected upon his party career:

> The party with which I acted had, by the malevolent and unthinking, been reproached, and by the wise and good always esteemed and confided in – as an aristocratic Party. Such I always understood it to be in the true sense of the word. I understood it to be a Party, in its composition and in its principles connected with the solid permanent long possessed property of the Country . . . attached to the ancient usages of the Kingdom, a party, therefore essentially constructed upon a ground plot of stability and independence.[57]

In relating his theory of party so closely to the Whig aristocracy Burke has laid himself open to the charge not only that he was behaving obsequiously towards the Lords of the Rockingham party but that he was attempting to reduce the influence of the crown in order to strengthen that of the aristocracy. Had Burke ever troubled to reply to this charge he would have pointed out that such a transfer of power would not have damaged the constitution, that it would only have served more strongly to safeguard the rights of the people, and that it would have corrected the balance of the constitution which had been upset by the activities of the court cabal in recent years. Burke is, perhaps, more open to criticism for his unquestioning acceptance of the divine right of the owners of hereditary property to govern the country. He did not defend the principle; he regarded it as self-evident, not troubling to inquire into the status of inherited privilege, still less to question the humanity, justice and efficiency of aristocratic government. His failure to do so is striking. For Burke knew the aristocracy well. Indeed, in his private correspondence he frequently criticized the leaders of his own party for their irresponsibility, their laziness, their inattention to business, their short-sightedness and their

---

[55] *Works*, II, 246.   [56] Ibid., 238.
[57] Burke to William Weddell, 31 January 1792, loc. cit.

selfishness. Why, then, should he so readily have allowed them the enormous responsibility of governing the country?

The answer is that there appeared to be no dispute about the matter. The Whigs had been the party and Whiggism had been the creed of government for half a century when Burke wrote. Yet to justify the political activities and to defend the principles of the Rockingham Whigs it was necessary for Burke to convert an ideology of government into an ideology of opposition. This he did by reviving the pre-Walpolean 'country' aspects of Whiggism which had placed considerable emphasis upon limiting the royal authority and stressing the popular responsibilities of political power. Both of these objectives could safely be achieved by the aristocracy acting through the agency of party. Party, for Burke, therefore, was not an end in itself. His primary intention was to restore the balance of the constitution. Party was only a means towards that end. In the same way, he did not defend aristocracy *per se*. Indeed, he once said of the aristocracy: 'I hold their order in cold and decent respect. I hold them to be of an absolute necessity in the Constitution; but I think they are only good when kept within their proper bounds.'[58]

We should not be misled by the fact that Burke leapt to the defence of popular liberties 'threatened' by the court for political reasons. He lived contentedly with the assumption that the opinions of the country, together with the affections and the confidence of the people, were represented by the landlords, who were the patrons, protectors and paternal guardians of the countless communities which together made up the kingdom. These men should lead the country and guide its opinions; they should not slavishly follow the transient whims of popular prejudice. Politics, and thus party, started and stopped with the aristocracy. Because he wished to maintain the unity of their order Burke did not believe it to be the business of politicians to legislate on contentious issues. Their business was to preserve the constitution by safeguarding its principles. Political action, for Burke, meant the removal of abuse not the implementation of a programme, the restoration of a theoretically ideal constitution, not a series of humanitarian reforms. For Burke, as we have been reminded, 'the programme of a party is to be found in its history . . . not in its plans for the future'.[59] Because of his preoccupation with precedent, therefore, Burke was uninterested in considering certain critically important constitutional

[58] Speech on the Repeal of the Marriage Act, 1781, *Speeches* (4 vols 1816), II, 279.
[59] Harvey Mansfield Junior, *Statesmanship and Party Government* (Chicago, 1965), 188.

issues with which party men might have to deal. He had, for example, little to say about the whole question of the relationship between the king, the ministers and parliament. He did not face up to the fact that there was an inherent contradiction between the conception of a party ministry and the royal prerogative of appointing ministers because he failed to conceive of the possibility that party might become a permanent part of the constitution.

We should not, however, allow critical observations to conceal the more positive aspects of Burke's theory of party. The notions of party and opposition once more obtained currency in the political language of the period. In establishing a measure of ideological unity for his party, Burke fashioned a theory out of the disparate experiences and prejudices of the Rockingham Whigs which, in its very ambiguity, permitted of flexible development at the hands of future generations. It is immaterial that his diagnosis of secret influence was hopelessly exaggerated. Historically, what matters is that his ideas took root in the minds of the Rockingham Whigs. That later generations credited Burke with the intellectual paternity of the two party system, however, is merely one of the paradoxes of modern British history, for Burke would have denied not only the paternity but perhaps also the legitimacy of the offspring.

After 1770 Burke slowly began to change his mind about party. Although on public occasions he continued to assert the indispensability of party, his private opinions began to diverge from his public utterances. In 1777, for example, he wrote to one of his closest friends in an unusually frank and delightfully sincere vein:

Also my dear friend those whom you and I trust, and whom the public ought to love and trust, have not that trust and confidence in themselves which their merits authorise, and which the necessities of the Country absolutely demand. . . . But still, as you say, they are our only hope; on my conscience, I think the best men, that ever were. We must therefore bear their infirmities for their virtues, and wait their time patiently. I believe you know that my chief employment for many years has been that woeful one, of a flapper. I begin to think it time to leave off. It (advice) only defeats its own purpose when given too long and too liberally; and I am persuaded that the men who will not move, when you want to teize them out of their inactivity, will begin to reproach yours, when you let them alone. Perhaps, they would not, after all, be so right; if one had in his own mind a distinct plan, when he could propose to others, and make it a point with them to pursue. I do not remember to have found myself at a loss in my own Mind about our Conduct, until now. I confess it; I do not know how to push others to resolution, whilst I am unresolved myself.[60]

It was not until 1780, however, that events first began seriously to weaken Burke's party attachment. In that year parliamentary reform first emerged as an issue which threatened to destroy the unity of the Rockingham party. Its acceptance by some of the party leaders horrified Burke. In 1780, too, he lost his prestigious seat at Bristol. He became even more dependent upon Rockingham, whose pocket borough of Malton he represented for the next fourteen years. Even when the Rockinghams returned triumphantly to power in 1782 Burke felt little jubilation. 'The Arrangement', he remarked, 'has not been wholly in Lord Rockingham's hands. But on the whole, things have turned out much better than could be expected.'[61] But not for him. 'I am a placeman of some rank; but have no share whatsoever, except what belongs to me a member of Parliament, in the conduct of public affairs.'[62] When Rockingham died in the summer of 1782 Burke was stunned. To the Marquis he had owed his career. Although he continued to support the party loyally his authority within it diminished and his ardour for the party battle declined. Although the infamous Fox–North coalition owed nothing to Burke it was he who retained most of the odium for the ill-fated India bill of 1783. After the disastrous general election of 1784, which resulted in about one hundred losses for the party of Fox and North, Burke had had enough of the fruitless party battle of which he had been the first casualty.

I consider the House of Commons as something worse than extinguished. We have been labouring for near twenty years to make it independent; and as soon as we had accomplished what we had in View, we found that its independence led to its destruction. The people did not like our work, and they joined the Court to pull it down. The demolition is very complete. Others may be more sanguine; but for me to look forward to the Event of another twenty years toil – it is quite ridiculous. I am sure the Task was more easy at first than it is now. The examples which have been made must operate. I can conceive that men of spirit might be persuaded to persevere in a great and worthy undertaking for many years, at the hazard, and even with the certainty of the utmost indignation of a Court; but to become Objects of that indignation only to expose

[60] Burke to William Baker, 12 October 1777, *Correspondence*, III, 388–9.
[61] Burke to John Lee, 25 March 1782, ibid., IV, 427.
[62] Burke to John Hely Hutchinson, *post*-9 April 1782, ibid., 440–1.

themselves to popular indignation, and to be rejected by both Court and Country, is more perhaps than any one could expect, certainly a great deal more than one will meet, except perhaps in three or four men, who will be more marked for their singularity and obstinacy, than pitied for their feeble good intentions.[63]

This was the end of Burke's consistent and continuous party campaigning. He continued to support the party of Fox but his energies were involved in issues which transcended party, such as the impeachment of Warren Hastings, the question of Ireland and, of course, the French revolution. Nevertheless he continued to believe in the doctrine of party although he left others to undertake the detailed work which he had outlined in the later 1760s. After the outbreak of war between Britain and revolutionary France, however, Burke became increasingly indifferent to party politics, feeling, as he did that European civilization was endangered by the contagion of atheistic Jacobinism. Shortly before his death, he was convinced that a new and dangerous polarity existed in politics. The old parties had become defunct:

... these parties, which by their dissensions have so often distracted the kingdom, which by their union have once saved it, and which by their collusion and mutual resistance have preserved the variety of this constitution in its utility, be (as I believe they are) nearly extinct by the growth of new ones, which have their roots in the present circumstances.[64]

In this crisis, the old party conflicts must be forgotten. Whigs and Tories should unite against the common enemy, the Jacobins. Much to Burke's satisfaction, the larger part of Fox's party formed a coalition with the Younger Pitt in 1794. Only a rump of the Whigs remaining loyal to him, Fox endured over a decade of fruitless opposition. In effect, party was dead.[65] Although in a subtle way, the old Whig party continued to exist as a refuge of moral and political principle,[66] in practice, the party no longer mattered.

To what extent the party of Rockingham and of Fox had been able to achieve what Burke had intended for it is not easy to decide. His own personal and political disappointments, the death of Rockingham

[63] Burke to William Baker, 22 June 1784, *Correspondence*, V, 154.
[64] Speech on the Quebec Act, 11 May 1791, *The Parliamentary History*, XXIX, 421.
[65] The Foxite Whigs numbered only about 50–60 members of parliament in the period 1794–1804, the only group in systematic opposition to the conservative coalition which governed Britain during the revolutionary period.
[66] Burke to Lord Fitzwilliam, 2 September 1796, loc. cit.

in 1782 and the military crisis of the 1790s had obscured the natural operations of party. What Burke had described in 1769–70 as the only means of saving the country had become a political luxury which the safety of the constitution could not afford. The significance of Burke's idea of party, however, does not end with the apparent disappointment of Burke's party expectations. It provided the starting point for Burke's analysis of the British constitution; it elicited from him a wide ranging discussion of the nature of the British polity. The party situation of the Rockingham Whigs, in fact, forced Burke to reinforce his party notions with a new Whig theory of the British constitution.

Chapter II

The British Constitution

The supreme practicality of Burke's thought is nowhere better illustrated than in his solicitousness to explain – and in explaining, to defend – the British constitution. At all times he was moved by political considerations in his theoretical activities. Early in his political career he placed his party philosophy within a framework of constitutional ideas. This he proceeded to define under the pressure of circumstances, especially the campaigns for economical and parliamentary reform. Later, Burke defended the British constitution from the Jacobins at home and abroad in such works as *Reflections on the Revolution in France* (1790) and the *Appeal from the New to the Old Whigs* (1791). Not only were Burke's inquiries always undertaken for pressing political reasons; they were directed towards the solution of practical questions, such as the degree of representation or the extent of toleration permissible within the British state. Burke was uninterested for the most part, in such theoretical questions as the location and distribution of sovereignty in the state.

His lack of interest does not only arise from his personal dislike of abstract inquiries; for him, such questions were already and unalterably settled. Sovereignty, for example, was vested in king and parliament. Burke did not regard the British constitution as perfect; he nevertheless looked upon it as perfect for Englishmen. He viewed it as the product of the ages, as a fully developed and fully matured entity rather than as a continually changing political structure. To understand fully this idiosyncratic conception of the British state it will be useful to examine the sub-structure of socio-economic considerations from which his political theory arose.

Burke had been interested in economics since his student days and had acquired both first-hand experience and specialist knowledge of the subject during his years in his native country in the sixties. His reviews in the *Annual Register* showed a keen appreciation of economics. (He reviewed Adam Smith's *Theory of Moral Sentiments*

favourably in 1759.) In these early days Burke adopted some fundamental axioms from which he never subsequently moved. He accepted
the socio-economic framework without question. His deep conviction
of the value of class harmony and social cohesion overrode any considerations of popular rights which he may have entertained. For
Burke, the poor were both too ignorant and too numerous to aspire
to economic or political power. Social inequality held no terrors for
Burke. In fact, it was part of the natural order of things. There was no
difference of *interest* between the rich and the poor because the rich
act as the trustees of the poor, as their protectors and as their providers,
taking, in their profits, a just commission for these responsibilities.
Inequality also had an historical vindication. Burke wrote of 'the
inequality, which grows out of the *nature of things* by time, custom,
succession, accumulation, permutation and improvement of property'.
Such inequality was, for Burke, 'much nearer that true equality,
which is the foundation of equity and just policy, than any thing
which can be contrived by the Tricks and devices of human skill'.[1]
Burke would not therefore seriously entertain the possibility that a
conflict of interest could arise between the producer and the consumer,
the employer and the labourer, the rich and the poor, that could not
be settled by some mutually acceptable and equitable compromise. As
he put it towards the end of his life:

> There is an implied contract, much stronger than any instrument,
> or article of agreement between the labourer in any occupation and
> his employer, that the labourer, so far as that labour is concerned,
> shall be sufficient to pay to the employer a profit on his capital and a
> compensation for his risk.[2]

Burke therefore, regarded society as a self-regulating mechanism, a
totality in which harmony could be found even in the most unequal
of relationships.

Social harmony was not thus the product of government intervention.
It was a function of the market. Governments ought not to interfere
with its operations for the market was governed by mysterious,
beneficent laws which steadied prices, allowed just profits and, indirectly, protected property. Government regulation which depressed
prices artificially would both impoverish the manufacturer and lead
to unemployment. Government regulation to raise wages would have
the same effect. On the other hand, regulation either to raise prices or

[1] Edmund Burke to John Bourke, November 1777, *Correspondence*, III,
402–4.
[2] *Works*, VII, 380 (*Thoughts and Details on Scarcity*).

reduce wages would have equally unfortunate results: the reduction of demand and the creation of unemployment. From these rough and ready and perfectly commonplace notions Burke was to construct a non-interventionist philosophy of government in which the role of the executive was limited and in which far-reaching and theoretical schemes of political and social reform thus became quite irrelevant. From these basic notions, too, Burke was to devise an imperial outlook which limited the role of the British parliament, permitting colonial commerce, left to itself, to flourish. There was thus nothing idealistic or utopian about Burke's view of government and society. Much of it, indeed, was little more than a reflection and a refinement of contemporary attitudes. For Burke gave an enormous presumptive advantage to existing institutions. He was not prepared to be over-critical of them if, in general, they were able to achieve the limited aims which he set for them.

Burke was thus much more concerned with the presumptive rights of government than with theoretical discussions of the origins or the nature of government. The origins of government, indeed, were not to him a matter of practical concern. He wrote little about them before the 1790s and, even then, refused to say anything very significant on the subject:

> The foundations on which obedience to government is founded are not to be constantly discussed. That we are here, supposes the discussion already made and the dispute settled. We must assume the rights of what represents the public to controul the individual, to make his acts and his will to submit to their will, until some intolerable grievance shall make us know that it does not answer its end, and will submit neither to reformation or restraint. Otherwise we should dispute all the points of morality, before we can punish a murderer, robber and adulterer.[3]

That there attaches a clear, presumptive right in favour of established institutions is a proposition which Burke does not find it necessary to demonstrate further. The functions of government itself are determined by the practical needs of the state and, for Burke, they should be confined

> to what regards the state, or the creatures of the state, namely, the exterior establishment of its religion; its magistracy; its revenue; its military force by sea and land; the corporations that owe their existence to its fiat; in a word, to everything that is truly and *properly*

[3] *Works*, X, 51–2 (Speech on the Unitarians Petition, 11 May 1792).

public, to the public peace, to the public safety, to the public order, to the public prosperity.[4]

This amounted to little more than the state's right to perpetuate itself and its institutions. There was no hint here of social reform, no intimation of consulting the wishes of the people, no conception of a changing or developing polity. The function of government was to preserve the state and its institutions. Necessary adjustments, adaptations and changes might occur but, ultimately, existing institutions must survive.

This first duty of government, however, was not a matter of legislation:

> Nations are not primarily ruled by laws; less by violence. Whatever original energy may be supposed either in force or regulation; the operation of both is, in truth, merely instrumental. Nations are governed by the same methods, and on the same principles, by which an individual without authority is often able to govern those who are his equals or his superiors; by a knowledge of their temper, and by a judicious management of it; I mean, – when public affairs are steadily and quietly conducted; not when Government is nothing but a continued scuffle between the magistrates and the multitude; in which sometimes the one and sometimes the other is uppermost; in which they alternatively yield and prevail, in a series of contemptible victories, and scandalous submissions.[5]

Indeed, Burke did not think about *government* as some of his contemporaries did, as the application of the maxims of jurisprudence and statecraft to particular situations. Burke did not regard government as a science. He had an elevated conception of the art of politics and saw it as a process which required the exercise of all the great qualities of the human mind[6] whose aim was to secure the confidence of the governed as a step towards pursuing 'the interest and desire of common prosperity'. How this in all circumstances was to be achieved was a problem of statesmanship. Until the period of the French Revolution Burke had little to say about the theoretical aspects of politics. His silence on the subject can be accounted for in part because for many years his concerns were largely those of the practical politician whose interest focused upon the problems of Britain and the British Empire. In so far as Burke may be deemed to have professed a political theory

---

[4] *Works*, VII, 416 (*Thoughts and Details on Scarcity*).
[5] Ibid., II, 218–19 (*Thoughts on the Cause of the Present Discontents*).
[6] Speech on the Regulation of the Civil List, 15 February 1781, *Speeches*, I, 213.

of the state before the French revolution, therefore, it was a political theory of the British constitution.

One of the most fundamental assumptions of Burke's political theory derived from Bolingbroke. This was the assumption that the 'great parties' of the reign of Queen Anne were dead and with them the shibboleths of the time. The Glorious Revolution and the Revolution Settlement had together established a new concensual framework for British politics in which the party passions and party principles of the late seventeenth and early eighteenth centuries were no longer relevant to politics. The principles of traditional Whiggism ('The power and majesty of the people, an original contract, the authority and independency of Parliament, liberty, resistance, exclusion, abdication, depositions') and Toryism ('Divine, hereditary, indefeasible right, lineal succession, passive obedience, prerogative, non-resistance') no longer mattered.[7] Burke did not, therefore, adopt a two party distinction in his discussion of eighteenth-century politics, preferring to speak the customary language of the 'balance of the constitution'. Bolingbroke, indeed, had already attacked Walpole for using 'influence' to upset the balance of the constitution established at the Revolution. Walpole's scribblers had responded to such charges by pointing out that 'balance' did not mean the *separation* of the parts of the constitution. Influence, they argued, was necessary to make the parts of the constitution work together. Government could not be carried on unless ministers were permitted some influence over the deliberations of the lower house. Although Burke used such language and adopted such concepts he did not think in mechanistic terms of the balanced constitution. Early in his career he thought in terms of a confrontation between the crown and the aristocracy, and, later in his career, in terms of a confrontation between the people and the aristocracy.

In the absence of organized parties, Burke's discussion of the balanced constitution inevitably considered the role of the monarch within it, and, in particular, as the repository of emergency and discretionary powers. Burke regarded this as a regrettable necessity, an outcome of the need to repose these powers *somewhere* out of the way of everyday political conflict. Furthermore, he insisted that these powers should be exercised upon public principles and national grounds. This could best be done by placing the exercise of these powers in the hands of the ministers. The just and proper influence of the crown – sufficient to maintain its dignity, to pay its household and to maintain itself in a manner appropriate to the national dignity –

[7] H. N. Fieldhouse, 'Bolingbroke and the Idea of Non-Party Government', *History*, XXIII (1938), 46.

this was acceptable to Burke. What he objected to was the influence of the crown being held out 'as the main and chief and only support of Government'.[8] Furthermore, he protested not merely against the increasing influence of the crown but also against the fact that this influence was falling into the wrong hands. Burke believed that the influence of the crown should be bestowed only upon the highest orders of men in the state but 'It has now insinuated itself into every creek and cranny in the kingdom'.[9] He feared that the purpose of 'influence' was being lost sight of – that of facilitating a political connection between the ministers and the Commons – as its volume increased.

Nevertheless, Burke spent the second half of his career fighting not the influence of the crown but the influence of the people. He fought the second rather more vigorously than he fought the first for the aristocratic power which he championed had more in common with royal power than with popular politics. Both rested upon traditional practices, established institutions, landed wealth and the distribution of offices and sinecures. Essentially, Burke believed that government ought to be in the hands of the aristocracy rather than in the hands of the people. The sober conduct of business, to say nothing of the independence of parliament, might be severely compromised if government had constantly to attend to the popular voice. In adopting this view, Burke was, consciously or not, echoing the elitist sentiments of Walpolean writers, echoes which reverberated in other, related, areas of Burke's thought, most particularly in his attitude towards parliament.

From a different and more philosophical, point of view, however, Burke argued that not only the Commons but all the political and legal institutions of the country had a popular origin. How does this relate to the anti-popular drift of so much of his thinking? Burke explained:

> The king is the representative of the people; so are the lords; so are the Judges. They are all trustees for the people, as well as the Commons; because no power is given for the sole sake of the holders.[10]

Furthermore, the popular aspects of government were not centred exclusively upon the lower house: 'although Government certainly is an institution of Divine authority, yet its forms and the persons who administer it, all originate from the people'.[11] The popular nature of

---

[8] Burke to Rockingham, 14 February 1771, *Correspondence*, II, 194.
[9] Speech on a Plan of Economical Reform, 15 December 1779, *Speeches*, II, 5.
[10] *Works*, II, 288 (*Thoughts on the Cause of the Present Discontents*).
[11] Ibid.

the House of Commons could not, therefore be gainsaid. The House could only fulfil its proper political objectives of exercising vigilance over the executive and giving expression to the grievances of the people if it reflected 'the express image of the feelings of the nation'.[12] The Commons, therefore, was the most important part of the constitution. This was one more reason why Burke, although he accepted the rights of the crown, the Lords, and the Commons, could not accept the idea of a precise balance of their respective powers, for balance implied equality.

These principles Burke regarded as fixed and unchanging, beyond the power of man to alter or amend. It was for this reason, among others, that he criticized the ministerial attack upon the rights of electors in 1768–9.[13] He did not accuse the ministers of acting illegally. Indeed, what they had done was not self-evidently illegal but, equally self-evidently, what they had done operated against the spirit of the constitution itself, a factor which transcended questions of legality.

> We do not *make* laws. No; we do not contend for this power. We only *declare* law; and, as we are a tribunal both competent and supreme, what we declare to be law becomes law, although it should not have been so before.[14]

There exist powers beyond and outside the laws with which the law and with which parliament may not tamper. The rights of electors were among these rights, whose exercise was essential to the proper identity of the lower house. It was beyond the competence of that house to change its own nature, although this was what the ministers were effectively seeking to achieve. In exactly the same way, Burke retrospectively criticized George III's elevation of Bute, a minister who had no connection with the people and who owed his office to court favour alone. Burke did not consider the possibility that such a minister might have just as wise a conception of the public good as a minister given by the people to the king. For Burke, what was important was that a minister must come to power on public and national rather than on private grounds.

Burke frequently adverted, therefore, to a standard of judgement whose criterion is how far parliament is able to maintain its historic character. For example, Burke condemned the court system and its 'rule of indiscriminate support to all Ministers'[15] because it weakened the function of the Commons as a check upon the executive. It prevented parliament from exercising its right to withhold support from govern-

---

[12] *Works*, II, 228. [13] See above, p. 24.
[14] *Works*, II, 303 (*Thoughts on the Cause of the Present Discontents*). [15] Ibid., 290.

ment 'until power was in the hands of persons who were acceptable to the people'.[16] Burke's thinking operated permanently, therefore, within the classical eighteenth-century framework of king, parliament and people. He did not envisage a dynamic and changing political system. He was content to allow the various parts of the constitution to perpetuate themselves. His constitutional crusades sought to *restore* to parliament its original characteristics. Burke protested against the innovation of 'the rule of indiscriminate support to all ministers' because it threatened to change the nature of parliament and although it was not illegal through precedent it *must* be illegal of its nature. Anything which weakened the essential characteristics of parliament, such as its control over its own membership, its necessary connection with the opinions of the people, *must* be illegal. This is clear enough and explains why Burke regarded certain actions as illegal. But what gave to the constitution the enormous authority and prestige with which Burke credited it ? The answer can be found in Burke's idea of prescription.

His conception of prescription validated the titles to authority of existing institutions by their use and longevity. Unlike the Natural Law philosophers, Burke was uninterested in the original titles to authority or even property. For Burke, usage alone validated a title. (For earlier thinkers the *manner* in which property and power had been acquired had been an important element in establishing title.) Prescription slots neatly into Burke's philosophy for it legitimized the property and the powers of the heirs of the Glorious Revolution; it protected their property from seizure either by the crown or by the people. Prescription became a bulwark of aristocratic privilege at the hands of Burke. Property became sacrosanct. The propertied basis of aristocracy, indeed, of British society, rested upon a prescriptive foundation.[17] He specifically denied that the British constitution rested upon a Natural Law foundation because 'it is a prescriptive constitution, whose sole authority is, that it has existed time out of mind'.[18] And it is not only the authority of the constitution but the distribution of power within it which can claim such a prescriptive authority. 'Your king, your lords, your judges, your juries, grand and little, all, are prescriptive.'[19] How did Burke try to prove this assertion ? He proceeded from the observation that because it was not then known how parliament had come into existence, it was the *fact* of its coming into existence together with the fact of its survival which demonstrated the plausibility

[16] *Works*, II, 261 (*Thoughts on the Cause of the Present Discontents*).
[17] Ibid., X, 96 (Speech on Parliamentary Reform, 7 May 1782).
[18] Ibid.   [19] Ibid.

of the idea of a prescriptive constitution. Prescription had its peculiar attractions for Burke because it was,

> . . . an idea of continuity which extends in time as well as in numbers and in space . . . a deliberate election of ages and of generations; it is a constitution made by what is ten thousand times better than choice, it is made by the peculiar circumstances, occasions, tempers, dispositions, and moral, civil, and social habitudes of the people, which disclose themselves only in a long space of time.[20]

It was not difficult for Burke to relate the social function and the hereditary property of the aristocracy to the principle of prescription. He once wrote of the aristocracy that, 'their houses become the public repositories and offices of Record for the constitution' which had been safeguarded as much by the 'traditionary politics of certain families as by anything in the Laws and order of the State'.[21] This did not dispense with the law because the accumulation of property itself provoked envy: 'But still we must have laws to secure property; and still we must have ranks and distinctions and magistracy in the state, notwithstanding their manifest tendency to encourage avarice and ambition.'[22] Prescription, therefore, brought stability and order both to society and to politics. In particular, prescription underpinned the framework of the social order which made both rights and duties possible in a civilized society. Liberty might be an integral element in the political and constitutional structure of Great Britain. Prescription was its very foundation.

Burke's doctrine of prescription was translated into the circumstances of the British constitution and applied to the ideology of Whiggism. Not that Burke concerned himself with the speculative niceties of Whig doctrine. It was not his manner to involve himself in sterile controversies. His definition of Whiggism was almost platitudinous: the promotion of 'the common happiness of all those, who are in any degree subjected to our legislative Authority; and of binding together in one common tie of Civil Interest, and constitutional Freedom, every denomination of Men amongst us'.[23] Ambiguous his formulation of Whiggism may have been but it played a vital role in his thought. The most important aspect of Whiggism, for Burke, was its prescriptive aspect: the idea of hereditary trusteeship. Burke had written in the *Thoughts* that

---

[20] *Works*, X, 97.
[21] Burke to the Duke of Richmond, 15 November 1772, *Correspondence*, II, 372–8.
[22] *Works*, X, 140 (Speech on the Repeal of the Marriage Act, 1781).
[23] Burke to John Noble 24 April 1778, *Correspondence*, III, 437–78.

government originates with the people and that it should be conducted on public rather than on private grounds; nevertheless he refused to admit the people to any share in government. This did not mean that the wishes, still less, the interests of the people should not be consulted. Political power should be held in trust for them: 'The king is the representative of the people; so are the lords, so are the judges. They are all trustees for the people, as well as the Commons, because no power is given for the sole sake of the holder.'[24] One aspect of Burke's conception of prescription, therefore, is that of hereditary responsibility. Burke's veneration of the historic process constantly underpinned his unswerving concern for the preservation of the prescriptive constitution. For Burke, the hereditary aristocracy acted as the repository of the accumulated experience of time, as trustees for the values and the wisdom of the community.

The notion of trusteeship, however, did not remain an exclusive and narrow conception. Burke gave it new vigour and a new relevance by investing it with some of the newer humanitarian elements which were beginning to dissolve the old political certainties. Burke revived Whiggism. To men of his generation, he must have appeared to be a man of advanced opinions, believing as he did not only in limited monarchy and government by consent, but in social justice, social harmony, liberty, religious toleration and the reform of government. The framework of Whig trusteeship was traditional. Its content was modern. The great message of Edmund Burke – that power was to be exercised on behalf of the people – needed reasserting after two generations of aristocratic rule. To grasp the significance of Burke's notion of trusteeship allows one to escape from the sterile discussions concerning Burke's 'consistency'. To understand that notion throws light on the simple fact that both Burke's early defence of parliament and people and his later defence of authority were simply different methods of resisting attacks upon aristocratic trusteeship.[25] The enormous responsibilities which rested upon politicians arose directly from the heavy powers and obligations with which they had been invested. The politician was the servant, in some ways, the agent, of society and property. He did not exist to serve his own purposes.

One of the most famous and influential aspects of Burke's political philosophy flows logically from his concept of trusteeship, his idea of representation. For Burke, representation, did not involve, quite

[24] See above, p. 50.
[25] Perhaps Burke's deep religious feelings and passionate humanitarian instincts were the crucial characteristics of his philosophy which rescued it from the dull sterility of so much contemporary thought.

literally, the representing of all people, places and interests in the kingdom. Rather it involved doing justice to all on the grounds of the general good and the public welfare.

> Virtual representation is that in which there is a communion of interests, and a sympathy in feelings and desires between those who act in the name of any description of people, and the people in whose name they act, though the trustees are not chosen by them.[26]

The representative system was not, therefore, primarily a mechanism for registering the opinions of the country. It was first and foremost the arena for reconciling different interests in the state. Although political power must be exercised for the good of the people, it ought to be exercised neither by them nor under their surveillance. 'I shall always follow the popular humour, and endeavour to lead it to right points, at any expence of private Interest, or party Interest, which I consider as nothing in comparison.'[27] But Edmund Burke would never allow the crowd to choose his principles for him.

The best known part of Burke's attitude towards representation is his conception of the duty of a member of parliament. It would be well, however, to make two cautionary statements. One is that his conception did not achieve the fame and prominence for contemporaries that it did for subsequent generations. The other is that Burke was arguing for the independence of an MP not only from his constituents but also from his patron or patrons. Burke faced the practical problem of relations between himself and his constituents while he represented Bristol from 1774 to 1780. For the rest of his career Burke's relations with his patrons, Verney, Rockingham and Fitzwilliam were more important than those with his constituents. Yet Burke believed that an MP ought 'to live in the strictest union, the closest correspondence and the most unreserved communication with his constituents'.[28] Furthermore, the wishes of his constituents 'ought to have great weight with him; their opinions high respect; their business unremitted attention', but he should not sacrifice to them 'his unbiased opinion, his mature judgement, his enlightened conscience'. In the last analysis, these faculties should be exercised at the discretion of the member. Burke asserted that 'They are a trust from providence, for the abuse

[26] *Works*, VI, 360 (Letter to Sir Hercules Langrishe, 1792).
[27] Burke to the Duke of Portland, 3 September 1780, *Correspondence*, IV, 274.
[28] *Works*, III, 18 (Speech at the conclusion of the Poll, Bristol, 1774). For Burke's activities as MP for Bristol see P. Underdown, 'Edmund Burke, the Commissary of his Bristol Constituents, 1774–80', *English Historical Review* (1954) where the author demonstrates the very great industry which he expended on behalf of his constituents.

of which he is deeply answerable' because government was not a matter of will but 'of reason and judgement, not of inclination'. And he stated in famous words that parliament was 'not a *congress* of ambassadors from hostile and different interests' but 'a deliberative assembly of *one* nation, with *one* interest, that of the whole' in which 'the general good, resulting from the general reason of the people' should prevail.[29] Burke, therefore, believed that members must not act purely from local or from sectional considerations but 'upon a *very* enlarged view of things'. Burke, as will have become apparent by now, was more concerned to represent the best interests of the people rather than their opinions. The two need not, of course, be the same. 'I maintained your interest, against your opinions', he proudly told his Bristol constituents.

It was, to say the least, slightly perverse for Burke to declare his indifference to the opinions of his constituents at just that moment in history when, after half a century of apathy, the constituencies were once again beginning to stir. In the same way, it was perhaps unwise for Burke to begin to idealize the representative system of the age and to ignore the glaring abuses within it at just that moment when voices were being raised demanding its extensive reform. Burke's theory of representation had much to do with the fact that the Rockingham Whigs were unable effectively to co-operate with the radicals who demanded the reform of parliament as doggedly as Burke and the Rockinghams constantly rejected it. Burke, with all his talk of trusteeship, ignored the wishes of the people whenever it suited him to do so. Public opinion, for example, clearly supported a coercive policy towards America but the Rockingham Whigs opposed coercion. Here was a gulf of sentiment between the Rockingham Whigs and the people. Here was a breakdown in Burke's 'logic'. For it was possible to explain away the huge majorities which Lord North continued to enjoy as the operation of royal influence corrupting members of parliament but it was scarcely possible to indict a whole people as corruptible. Burke was painfully aware of the fact that it was impossible to change the public mood. Only a military disaster in America could effect such a transformation.

By the mid seventies it was clear that his suggested panacea for the 'Present Discontents', party, had not succeeded in attaining the objectives which Burke had laid down for it. This realization however, did not lead Burke to embrace ideas of radical reform.

You know how many are startled with the idea of innovation.

---

[29] *Works*, III, 360–1 (Speech previous to the Election, Bristol, 1780).

Would to God it were in our power to keep things *where they are*, in point of form; provided we are able to improve them in point of Substance. The Machine itself is well enough to answer any good purpose provided the Materials were sound.[30]

Long before the French Revolution revealed starkly to Burke the excesses to which innocently motivated reform could run, he had already pronounced his stern refusal to tamper with the framework of the constitution or to admit a reform which effected even the slightest change in the hierarchical structure of society and politics. He constantly deplored the fact that reformers 'turned their thoughts towards a change in the Constitution, rather than towards a correction of it in the form in which it now stands'.[31] He not only resisted but resented the climate of opinion which fostered attacks upon existing institutions. He was fond of ridiculing the parliamentary reformers for their attacks upon the House of Commons, the freest and most representative part of the constitution, while they neglected the Lords. He poured scorn upon radical fantasies about the 'Anglo-Saxon constitution', preferring to derive his own notions of reform from the known history of the constitution. As he once put it: 'I will not take their *promise* rather than the *performance* of the constitution.'[32] Burke detested radicals. He thought them unreliable, treacherous men who had no stake in the country, whose rantings threatened the principle that political power should be closely related to the ownership of property. He profoundly suspected their motives:

I like a clamour whenever there is an abuse. . . . But a clamour made merely for the purpose of rendering the people discontented with their situation, without an endeavour to give them a practical remedy, is indeed one of the worst acts of sedition.[33]

Fundamentally, as Burke admitted to the Commons in 1779 'I am . . . cautious of experiment, even to timidity, and I have been reproached for it.'[34] Yet by the end of the 1770s the failure of his party schemes to have the effects he had desired persuaded even Burke to take up the cause of reform.

The only type of constitutional reform which Burke thought to be permissible in the context of the English political system was economical

---

[30] Burke to Joseph Harford, 27 September 1780, *Correspondence*, IV, 294–9.
[31] Burke to Joseph Harford, 4 April 1780, ibid., IV, 218–22.
[32] *Works*, X, 101 (Speech on Parliamentary Reform, 7 May 1782).
[33] Ibid., 127 (Speech on the Juries Bill, 1771).
[34] Ibid., II, 7 (Speech on Economical Reform, 15 December 1779).

reform[35] undertaken by the Rockingham Whig aristocracy. Legislation would curb the opportunities for corruption and thus limit the ever-present threat of increasing royal influence. At the same time, it would safeguard the independence of parliament and enable it to act as a control both upon the crown and the people. Although economical reform had a respectable history in the Rockingham party stretching back to 1768 it was only brought forward as a comprehensive party policy late in 1779. That it should have been so was itself interesting. It indicated that Burke and his party only dared to take a reforming initiative if they were sure of enjoying the support of a public opinion which might otherwise have been seduced by the parliamentary reformers. The disasters of the American war, the growing paralysis of North's ministry and Britain's virtual helplessness against the Bourbon powers in Europe enabled the Rockinghams to bring forward their great plan for economical reform.

Burke entertained the highest expectations of his plan of economical reform, hoping that it would reduce the influence of the crown and strengthen the role of parliament, and especially the Commons, in the constitution. Yet, to be effective, Burke thought, the reform must be moderate; only by being so could it be permanent. It was not for self-educated reformers to tear up by the roots hallowed institutions which had stood the test of time and which were capable of still further development. Burke's position can easily be misrepresented. It was not his intention blindly to preserve *any* institution. He never denied that change was an integral part of the social process. The British constitution, which he so greatly admired, was itself the product of ages of growth, change and development. But what Burke *did* deny was that the essential principles upon which the constitution had been founded should ever be threatened by the hasty experiments of radical reformers. Economical reform contained none of these dangers. It offered one considerable attraction to Burke and his party. It was loudly demanded – and certain to be popular – in the country:

> I cannot indeed take upon me to say I have the honour to *follow* the sense of the people. The truth is, *I met it on the way*, while I was pursuing their interest, according to my own ideas.[36]

Economical reform was an old cry of the country party. It was not the invention of the radicals of the age of the American Revolution. It went back to the reign of Anne. To espouse the cause of economic reform was the natural reaction of an opposition party. But it is

---

[35] Strictly speaking, to attain cheaper and thus less corrupt government.
[36] Speech on Economical Reform, 11 February 1780, *Speeches*, II, 23–4.

significant that Burke had not been among those members of the Rockingham party who had earlier taken up the cry for economical reform.[37] The demand for economy, retrenchment, the ending of corruption – these were all among the platitudes of contemporary political discussion. It is too frequently forgotten that none other than George III came to the throne in 1760 with a bundle of naive intentions which are not dissimilar to the main planks of the economic reform platform. Given, therefore, the military disasters of the years 1777–9 and the rapidly worsening economic situation in the country it was almost natural for both public opinion and an opposition party which had inherited many of the 'country' slogans of the reign of Queen Anne to revert to the customary cures for the ills of the constitution.

Burke was always careful, however, to keep the popular tumult under the guidance of sober members of the landed class, and, in particular, of course, of the more substantial members of his own party. Such leadership of the popular movement would ensure that the constitution was saved:

> Is not every one sensible how much authority is sunk? The reason is perfectly evident. Government ought to have force enough for its functions, but it ought to have no more. It ought not to have force enough to support itself in the neglect, or the abuse of them. If it has, they must be as they are, abused and neglected. . . . The minister may exist but the government is gone.[38]

Economical reform was necessary, therefore, in the interests of good government in the long run, as well as in the interests of healing the divisions and curing the abuses in the state in the short.

Burke proposed in 1779 to abolish superfluous offices and outdated jurisdictions and franchises, proceeding on the principle that 'when the reason of old establishments is gone, it is absurd to preserve nothing but the burthen of them'.[39] Parliamentary scrutiny was to diminish wastefulness and reduce extravagance on the Civil List. This alone, according to Burke's sanguine prediction, would save 'a quantity of influence equal to the places of fifty members of parliament'.[40] What he was prepared to reform, however, was, in some

[37] It had, in fact, been the ex-Tory, William Dowdeswell, who had launched this little known campaign in 1768–70.
[38] Speech on Economical Reform, 15 December 1779, *Speeches*, II, 6.
[39] Speech on Economical Reform, 11 February 1780, *Speeches*, II, 22–8 for Burke's discussion of the principles upon which he based his economical reform bills.
[40] Speech on Economical Reform, 15 December 1779, *Speeches*, II, 8.

ways, less significant than what he was not. He had no intention of reducing the personal influence of the monarch. 'The crown shall be left an ample and liberal provision for personal satisfaction.'[41] Furthermore he did not propose to wield his reforming axe upon the pensions granted by the monarch on grounds of merit. Rewards for political service remained in the gift of the king. Essentially, Burke did not propose to change fundamentally the role of the monarch in the constitution and there remained the possibility that the king might still have the power to influence not only the personnel of the administration but also the proceedings of parliament. It was the abuse and the excesses of royal influence that Burke proposed to remove, not the influence of the crown in politics. Burke did not envisage a political system in which the crown counted for nothing. He did not conceive of novel government forms, still less did he embrace the notion of constitutional monarchy which became current in the nineteenth century. Indeed the conclusion is irresistible that Burke was less concerned to refashion the institutions of the state than he was to effect a timely reform which would quieten the popular tumult for radical reform.[42]

The political crisis of the years 1779–85, particularly the widespread demand in the country for radical change, forced Burke to define his attitude to parliamentary reform even more clearly than he had done in his writings of 1769 and 1770.[43] Burke – and the importance of the fact can hardly be exaggerated – was himself at the centre of a furious political storm in which the parliamentary reformers, especially those in Rockingham's own county of Yorkshire, demonstrated their dissatisfaction with economical reform. The division of opinion in his party between the parliamentary and the economic reformers deeply distressed Burke. For the first time he expressed a wish to retire from politics.[44] On the issue of parliamentary reform he would not compromise at all. He warned the Commons that the effects of extending the representation would be disastrous: 'either that the Crown by its constant stated power, influence, and revenue, would wear out all opposition in elections, or that a violent and furious popular spirit would arise'.[45]

We have already examined briefly the objections which Burke

[41] Ibid., 9.   [42] Ibid., 2.   [43] See above, pp. 36–7.
[44] For Burke's general political situation at this time, see N. C. Phillips, 'Edmund Burke and the County Movement', *English Historical Review*, LXXVI, 254–78.
[45] 8 May 1780, *The Parliamentary History*, XXI, 605.

raised in 1770 to proposals for the reform of parliament. To what extent had his views been affected by the reform movement of the later years of the American War of Independence? Were his private opinions of reform identical to his public utterances? In fact, his real opinions of reform were considerably more complicated than quotations, such as that given above, imply. For one thing, as is well known, he was fully aware of the obvious abuses in the electoral system of the day. For another, he was prepared, or so he said, to listen to the people for their opinions upon the desirability of reform: 'I most heartily wish that the deliberate sense of the kingdom on this great subject should be known. When it is known, it *must* be prevalent.'[46] Elsewhere, he stated that he was not opposed *in theory* to some change in the representation.[47] Perhaps Burke was trimming his sails to catch the winds of public opinion. Nevertheless, he denied that parliamentary reform *was* the wish of the people. Of shorter parliaments, he wrote, 'I do not know anything more *practically* unpopular.'[48] This was one way of escaping from the logical conclusion of his own admission. There was another. This was to set at naught the wishes of the people. In effect, Burke could say that he would follow the opinions of the people if those opinions were worth following. He had absolutely no intention of 'leaving to the Crowd, to choose for me, what principles I ought to hold, or what Course I ought to pursue for their benefit'.[49] What terrified Burke was the prospect, however remote, of a weak and unpopular government being rushed into ill thought out schemes of radical reform by the cries of the mob: 'They are men; it is saying nothing worse of them; many of them are but ill-informed in their minds, many feeble in their circumstances, easily overreached, easily seduced.'[50] It was thus the *consequences*, rather than the *principle*, of parliamentary reform which Burke abhorred.

Burke believed that government should exist for the good of the people but not that it should be controlled by the people. His firm belief that government should rest upon public principles did not mean that the people should be consulted constantly, 'as to the detail of particular measures, or to any general schemes of policy, they have neither enough of speculation in the closet, nor of experience in business, to decide upon it.[51] Burke's deep-rooted suspicion of the people must

---

[46] Burke to the chairman of the Buckinghamshire County Committee, 12 April 1780, *Correspondence*, IV, 226–9.
[47] Burke to Joseph Harford, 27 September 1780, loc. cit.   [48] Ibid.
[49] Burke to the Duke of Portland, 3 September 1780, loc. cit.
[50] *The Parliamentary History*, XXI, 607.
[51] *Works*, X, 76 (Speech on Sawbridge's Motion for Parliamentary Reform).

have been confirmed by three occurrences of the year 1780, just when there appeared to be *some* possibility, however remote, that his opinion might be on the point of change. The Gordon riots of June endangered the security of the capital for several days, an event which shocked and terrified large sections of the propertied classes of the nation. The parliamentary reformers whom Burke and his party had done much to conciliate only proceeded to oppose them in several constituencies in the general election of September. Finally, Burke's humiliation in losing his seat at Bristol at the election disillusioned him considerably. He had become the most famous casualty of the new force of public opinion. Burke's hostility to parliamentary reform, then, was neither so fanatical – at least before 1780 – nor so ideological as we tend to assume. Not surprisingly, his own political experiences played a large part in shaping and in confirming his opinions.

Perhaps our suggestion that Burke's hostility to parliamentary reform was neither so deep-rooted nor so 'ideological' as commentators have usually assumed is really not so surprising. After all, triennial parliaments had formed an integral part of the Revolution Settlement, which Burke always claimed to defend. (The Septennial Act could hardly be regarded as one of the fundamental laws of the constitution.) His argument that only the court would benefit from a wider franchise was nonsensical. A wider franchise would be likely to give considerable electoral advantages not to the court but to local patrons. Burke himself knew this very well.[52] But it does not seem to have occurred to him that it was exactly men like the Marquis of Rockingham who would have benefited from parliamentary reform, albeit at the cost of greater exertions and greater expenditure than they were accustomed to making. Burke's curious inconsistency on this subject was reflected yet again in his assertion that the constitution would not survive five triennial elections.[53] In the reigns of William and of Anne, however, the constitution had survived more than five triennial elections. His gloomy prognostications upon the likely effects of triennial parliaments, at least – and perhaps upon other reform proposals, too – should not be taken on their face value. It was ironical that in 1785, when Burke opposed Pitt's proposals to reform parliament, he was in the unaccustomed situation of defending George III against a reforming minister. Burke's hostility to parliamentary reform is enigmatic. But it is more than that. More than anything else it provides a link between the earlier part of his career when he was the liberal, party reformer, struggling to preserve freedom throughout the empire and the later

[52] *Works*, X, 78–9.   [53] Ibid., 83–7.

Burke who vigorously defended the established political system of Britain and Europe.

To depict Burke simply as the reactionary scourge of the radicals is, of course, to make a nonsense both of the man and his career. He was concerned not only with the defence of the political establishment but no less strongly with the defence and protection of the individual conscience. He addressed himself to this problem largely through the successive issues of religious toleration which agitated politics during the later eighteenth century. If it is fairly difficult to generalize with confidence about Burke's attitude to parliamentary reform, it is still less easy to pronounce with certainty upon his attitude to religious toleration. The reasons for this are many. First, it is not possible to find in his early writings much of a clue towards his later attitudes. Second, his ideas were set out unsystematically – as one might expect – in response to a series of unconnected issues and enunciated publicly when it may not be unfairly claimed that he may have been striving after rhetorical effect. Third, his ideas on toleration were neither systematic nor original. They derived from a variety of sources, especially from Locke. And although it is impossible to deny the presence in Burke's thought of certain recurring themes – the need to preserve the established church, the necessity of weighing with great caution the likely consequences of the slightest change in the church establishment, the wisdom of preserving a wide degree of freedom of opinion on religious matters – nevertheless, these do not constitute related aspects of a coherent theory of toleration. Indeed, his lack of system in this area of his thought is surprising. Before the 1790s, for example, he did not attempt a reasoned defence of the established church. His attitude towards the Anglican church was typically Burkean: it was an existing, workable institution which enjoyed a prescriptive right to endure. To this he attached a Lockian idea of the right of the individual to his own religious opinions. This kind of attitude was perfectly typical of the latitudinarian outlook of the period. Most contemporaries still accepted the right of the Anglican church to enjoy a privileged position in the state because of its landed wealth, its prestige and its status, its traditions of learning, theology and scholarship. Its privileged status need not, however, preclude a generous treatment of Dissenters, consistent with the security of the church. Burke reflected many of these attitudes. It was only when issues of religious toleration became matters of political controversy that he began to enunciate his own views upon toleration. That his ideas were formulated in this manner meant that they were inevitably rather less than systematic. Even one of the most consistent – and praiseworthy –

of his attitudes, his very real sympathy for the Irish Catholics, led him to adopt a view of toleration which was, in fact, inconsistent with other aspects of his political thought.

In the early 1770s a series of issues concerning toleration aroused Burke to express a somewhat inconsistent view of the rights of the individual measured against the rights of the church establishment. In 1772 certain Anglican clergymen petitioned parliament for relief from subscribing to the thirty-nine articles. He reacted in an extravagant and melodramatic manner. He criticized the petitioners for enjoying the benefits of establishment, accusing them of seeking preferment within an established church to whose basic rules they would not conform. 'Dissent', he bellowed, 'not satisfied with toleration, is not conscience but ambition.'[54] How could the grievances which the petitioners complained of be intolerable if they were not even suffered? For Burke, indeed, the question was not one of toleration. It was a question of safeguarding the church and the state. Once again, Burke invoked the principle of majority which later in his life he was thoroughly to repudiate. As a tactical ploy to reject the petition, Burke asserted that a lawful establishment could only be changed when a majority of the people living under it agrees that abuses have become intolerable.

On another occasion, however, Burke adopted a rather different principle: that the established church might make concessions if the extent of the relief demanded was insignificant. In 1772 certain Protestant Dissenters requested such a slight measure of relief. Burke, feeling that he could afford to be generous, declared that toleration should be an integral part of any establishment, claiming that the observances of the church were an accident of history rather than the creation of the Almighty.[55] To what a considerable extent, then, could Burke's religious thought be affected by the occasion which called it forth. In the same way, when the English Catholics petitioned for relief from the penal laws in 1780 Burke supported 'one of the most sober, measured, steady, and dutiful addresses that was ever presented to the crown'. And he affirmed that, in the emergency of war-time, 'the supreme power of the state should meet the conciliatory disposition of the subject'.[56]

Burke's ideas on toleration, in his earlier career, at least, lack both depth and coherence. His attitude towards the Irish Catholics arose,

[54] Speech on behalf of the Protestant Dissenters, 1772, *Speeches*, I, 108.

[55] This question of Burke's religious beliefs and observances entirely awaits detailed investigation. We know surprisingly little of his private, religious opinions and devotions.

[56] *Works*, III, 391 (Speech at Bristol Previous to the Election, 1780).

of course, not from his philosophy but from his background and his nationality. Indeed, he was prepared to concede to the Irish Catholics a far greater measure of toleration than he would have ever dreamed of allowing the English Dissenters. The reason for this almost certainly relates to the fact that his great objective in Irish affairs for many years was to reconcile to the Protestant Ascendancy the mass of Irish Catholics. Burke was thus not merely prepared to extend toleration but, indeed, to create in Ireland the kind of liberal society of which in other circumstances he was terrified. In the special case of Ireland, and in this case only, Burke was prepared to change existing institutions and customary practices. But how could he consistently defend such a proceeding? He could not, and therefore he invoked the Natural Law. It was safer to appeal to the Almighty than it was to assert the principle of majority. For Burke was prepared to concede to the Catholics the right to hold civil offices, to allow them the free and unhindered practice of their religion, to permit them to organize their own episcopate and to educate their own children. But may it not have been the case that the real impetus behind Burke's generosity was less the Natural Law than his profound fear that his fellow-countrymen might emulate the Americans unless their grievances were remedied in time?[57] Furthermore, Burke believed that he was not innovating. He was merely restoring to the Irish the rights which they had lost when they were deprived of their original constitution at the end of the seventeenth century. The *suspension* – for that was what it was – of the rights of the Irish Catholics was of too recent an origin to have acquired a prescriptive authority. With more truth than he perhaps realized Burke stated:

> I am perfectly indifferent concerning the pretexts under which we torment one another; or whether it be for the constitution of the Church of England, or for the constitution of the state of England, that people choose to make their fellow-creatures wretched. ... The diversified but connected fabric of universal justice is well cramped and bolted together in all its parts.[58]

But Edmund Burke's idea of toleration is not 'well cramped and bolted together in all its parts'. The same reservation may be made about his constitutional ideas in general. Even before the French Revolution wrought a great change in his thought on matters such as toleration, it is impossible to credit him with a coherent approach to

[57] In passing, it is worth remarking that Burke rarely, if ever, mentions the Natural Law during the 1770s either in British or imperial affairs.
[58] *Works*, III, 419 (Speech at Bristol previous to the Election, 1780).

political theory. He would allow one measure of toleration to one sort of Dissenter, a different measure to another, a completely different one to the Irish Catholics and in some cases hardly any relief at all. Such 'flexibility' can be accounted for by the circumstances in which he expounded his ideas – as we have remarked already – and by his commitment to a prescriptive idea of the British constitution. His concern for its preservation provoked him to express ideas in its defence which were not always strictly consistent with each other.

Burke's political philosophy may be described in many ways: as a – or the – Whig theory of the constitution; as the Whig doctrine of trusteeship; or as the theory of the balanced constitution. It lends itself to a variety of descriptions. But what it may not be described as is equally clear and much more important. It is not, and has little in common with, the modern doctrine of responsible government. Burke's thinking operated within the framework of the 'balanced' constitution of the eighteenth century. As we observed earlier, Burke sought to restore the old political order not to invent a new one. He completely failed to read the direction in which history was moving. The modern two-party system with alternating ministries, a prime minister, an impartial civil service and an apolitical monarch was completely unknown to – and unforeseen by – Burke, for he wished to restore the traditional constitution of the past, no less and no more.

Chapter III

The Imperial Problem: America

Edmund Burke's reactions to the imperial problems of his age, of America, of Ireland and of India, were seemingly indistinct and unconnected. The imperial statesman who preached conciliation with America appears to have little in common with the nationalist politician who strove to secure toleration for Irish Catholics or the great humanitarian who tried to reform the government of India. Burke's approach to imperial problems varied in time and according to the issue in hand. It is a large and dangerous assumption that Burke must have had a systematic, imperial 'theory'. It may be more rewarding however to examine Burke's general approach to problems of empire and the methodology he adopted in his imperial inquiries. Not surprisingly, his method was characterized by a fund of common-sense, practicality and a distaste for abstract theorizing. Burke never questioned the purpose of empire. He tacitly accepted Britain's *right* to her empire, her right to maintain it and to extend it. He assumed that the empire should (and did) bring peace, good government and justice to its inhabitants, according to the local conditions. He never entertained the opinion that only one type of administration would suit the diverse provinces of the emprie, 'I was never wild enough to conceive, that one method would serve for the whole; that the natives of Hindostan and those of Virginia could be ordered in the same manner.'[1]

Burke's method of treating the American problem was that of the practical politician rather than that of the speculative philosopher. He avidly consumed materials on the historical and political background of each colony. For Burke, imperial policy ought to derive partly from a statesmanlike awareness of history and experience but also from a prudential assessment of imperial interests throughout the British

[1] *Works*, III, 182 (Letter to the Sheriffs of Bristol, 1777).

67

dominions. He did not wish to concern himself with abstract rights, divorced from political, social and historical realities. He brought to bear upon imperial questions no set ideas and no preconceived notions. 'I was obliged to take more than common pains to instruct myself in everything which related to our colonies. I was not the less under the necessity of forming some fixed ideas concerning the general policy of the British empire.'[2] Indeed, his practical experience of the American problem included the period from December 1770 to August 1775 when he acted as colonial agent for the colony of New York, 'I think I know America. If I do not, my ignorance is incurable for I have spared no pains to understand it.'[3] Burke's imperial thinking, therefore, was not fixed and rigid; it grew with the problem itself.

In an age when the protection of property was the first duty of the law it was natural for men to think spontaneously in terms of *rights*; at such a time, the pragmatism of Burke was far more novel than we are inclined to assume. Although most of his contemporaries debated the American question in terms of the mother parliament's right to tax the colonists, Burke was prepared to ignore the question of right entirely, 'I am resolved this day to have nothing at all to do with the question of the right of taxation. Some gentlemen startle – but it is true; I put it totally out of the question. It is less than nothing in my consideration.'[4] The reasons for Burke's dislike of abstract discussion are clear: such discussions incited differences of opinion because abstract concepts could mean different things to different men. Solutions to political questions should be realistic proposals, not theoretical ideas or legalistic notions. It was not the way of man to 'follow up practically any speculative principle, either of government or of freedom, as far as it will go in argument or logical illation'. [*sic*][5] On the contrary: 'The question with me is, not whether you have a right to render your people miserable; but whether it is not your interest to make them happy. It is not what a lawyer tells me I *may* do; but what humanity, reason, and justice tell me I ought to do.'[6] Towards this end government must direct itself. He admitted without hesitation that:

> All government, indeed, every human benefit and enjoyment, every virtue, and every prudent act, is founded on compromise and barter. We balance inconvenience; we give and take; we remit some rights

---

[2] *Works*, III, 26 (Speech on Conciliation with America, 22 March 1775).
[3] Ibid., 160 (Letter to the Sheriffs).
[4] Ibid., 74 (Speech on Conciliation).   [5] Ibid., 110.   [6] Ibid., 75.

that we may enjoy others; and we choose rather to be happy citizens than subtle disputants.[7]

Not for Burke, then, the inflexible stand upon an absolute right. Every situation must be treated on its own merits. Furthermore, the statesman must not lose sight of the fact that men inevitably pursue their self-interest, 'Man acts from adequate motives relative to his interest; and not on metaphysical speculations.'[8] Men should not, however, be granted complete liberty to pursue their interests. As he put it: 'we must give away some natural liberty, to enjoy civil advantages'.[9]

Burke's approach to imperial questions, then, was exactly in line with his approach to political problems elsewhere. His philosophy proceeded from an acute perception of the realities of numan nature and the significance of history. It was with grim self-righteousness that Burke lectured his fellow members of parliament after the shattering news had reached Britain that the last army had surrendered in America. Parliament's blind enforcement of its imperial rights had almost ruined the country and now actually lost part of the empire.

> Oh, wonderful rights that are likely to take from us all that yet remains. What were those rights? Can any man describe them, can any man give them a body and soul answerable to all these mighty costs? We did all this because we had a right to do it: that was exactly the fact.[10]

We should pause here, however, to examine further Burke's undoubtedly sincere distaste for discussing abstract rights and his opposition to parliament's attempts to assert its rights. Viewed against the background of his party loyalties, Burke emerges less as the pragmatic statesman of empire than as the spokesman of the Rockingham Whig party. The leaders of the Rockingham party had been just as keen as the king and his supporters to maintain the rights of parliament over the colonies. The only difference between them had been that the Rockinghams had been more timid than other political groups in parliament in enforcing these rights. Here, then, was one powerful reason for Burke to avoid the discussion of such rights, for such a discussion would only have embarrassed the leaders of the Rockingham party. The Marquis of Rockingham himself had no intention of becoming embroiled in such discussions, and it was he who laid down the basic lines that not only Burke but the other Rockinghamite spokesmen such as Dowdesdell and Fox followed: that parliament had

---

[7] *Works*, III, 110–11.   [8] Ibid., 112.   [9] Ibid., 111.
[10] Speech at the Opening of the Session, 27 November 1781, *Speeches*, II, 288.

a customary right to tax the colonists 'but that such a right was irrelevant unless the Americans chose to acknowledge it'.[11]

Nevertheless Burke *did* uphold parliament's 'unimpaired and undiminished just, wise, and necessary constitutional superiority' and believed it to be 'consistent with all the liberties a sober and spirited America ought to desire'.[12] He had to accept that in law parliament had 'an unlimited legislative power over the colonies' which he wished to preserve 'perfect and entire'.[13] His objective, therefore, was 'To reconcile British superiority with American liberty.'[14] What Burke objected to was not so much parliament's right to tax but the extent to which parliament was prepared to go in enforcing its rights. He and his party differed from the North ministry over the question of coercing the colonies, a policy which was enforced with disastrous results in 1774. Thereafter it was Burke's intention to *restore* the traditional relationship which had hitherto existed between the Americans and the mother country: 'I propose, by removing the ground of the difference, and by restoring the *former unsuspecting confidence of the colonies in the mother country*'[15] to reconcile them to British rule. Burke continued to believe until the end of 1775 that a change of heart in London would be sufficient to revive the imperial relationship which had suffered such a profound shock on the field of Lexington[16] and hoped that a few concessions would satisfy men who had come to doubt the *raison d'être* of the British empire in North America (a popular contemporary fallacy). Such a fallacy probably had its origin in a tendency widespread amongst those in opposition to the North Ministry, to identify the Americans with the Whigs of 1688, the victims of oppression whose liberties were threatened by parliament's rigid insistence upon its rights. Their refusal to pay taxes to which they had not consented seemed reminiscent of the Whig resistance to James II. The Americans would return to their imperial allegiance as soon as the unjust taxes of which they complained were removed.

To some extent Burke understood this. Although he clung to his

[11] The Marquis of Rockingham to William Dowdeswell, 13 September 1774, Wentworth Woodhouse MSSRI-1504, Rockingham Papers, Sheffield Public Library. I wish to express my thanks to Earl Fitzwilliam and the Trustees of the Wentworth Woodhouse Estates for permission to quote from the Wentworth Woodhouse MSS.

[12] *Works*, III, 7 (Speech on Arrival at Bristol, 1774).

[13] Ibid., 177–8 (Letter to Sheriffs).

[14] Ibid., 7 (Speech on Arrival at Bristol).

[15] Ibid., 31 (Speech on Conciliation).

[16] In April 1775 an unimportant skirmish near Boston became the symbolic inauguration of the American struggle for independence.

belief in the supremacy of parliament and its right to tax the colonies, he believed that the levying of internal taxes might be undertaken by the Americans themselves, 'To mark the legal *competency* of the colony assemblies [sic] for the support of their givernment in peace, and for public aids in time of war.'[17] But what if the colonists refused to tax themselves? This was no difficulty for Burke. Taxation must be founded upon consent, otherwise the empire would become a military dictatorship. The Americans should not be taxed at all if they chose not to be. Their only connection with the mother country would then be the laws of trade, including the Navigation Acts, the commercial foundation of the empire. Burke's American thought, then led to his abandonment of the traditional concept of empire and its replacement by something approaching the modern idea of a free commonwealth of nations. He declared that the policy of taxing the colonists begun by George Grenville to be not only unprecedented but unwise and unnecessary.[18] The prosperity of the colonists in settled times would yield, in Burke's view, considerably more from external taxation than from internal dues such as the hated Stamp Tax. Such dues must be abandoned and the traditional bonds of imperial loyalty must be permitted to reassert themselves. Burke hoped for a voluntary, cultural attachment of the Americans to the mother country:

> My hold of the colonies is in the close affection which grows from common names, from kindred blood, from similar privileges, and equal protection. These are ties, which, though light as air, are as strong as links of iron. Let the colonies always keep the idea of their civil rights associated with your government, – they will cling and grapple to you; and no force under heaven will be of power to tear them from their allegiance.[19]

Burke did not believe that a policy of reconciliation would weaken the imperial authority of the British parliament. Such a policy was, indeed necessary to *restore* that authority and to maintain the empire.

Burke's conception of the integrity of the empire arose from his conviction that the imperial relationship must be voluntary. Between 1775 and 1777 his American thought developed rapidly as he sought constantly to relate it to a changing political and military situation. By the end of 1775 he was prepared to concede to the American congress the right of legislating for the colonies. Thereafter, he was

[17] *Works*, III, 92 (Speech on Conciliation).
[18] Ibid., 100–3.   [19] Ibid., 123–4.

prepared to concede almost anything so long as there remained the possibility, however remote, that some form (or even fiction) of imperial unity could be maintained. In the following year he had perforce to take into account the Declaration of Independence. Rejoicing in America's defiant struggle to maintain her liberties against the oppression of the British parliament, Burke lent his blessing to what he had been dreading for years – the separation of the colonies from the mother country. Burke justified this seeming inconsistency by extolling the beauties of liberty and freedom in the state which the Americans were striving to build for themselves.

The Declaration of Independence came as a blow for Burke for it had always been his primary objective to maintain the integrity of the empire. It came as an unwelcome surprise to him. He had underestimated the will of the colonists to resist the British. He said in his speech on conciliation: 'We thought . . . that the utmost which the discontented colonists could do, was to disturb authority; we never dreamt they could of themselves supply it.'[20] The outbreak of hostilities ended, he knew, 'all our prospects of American reconciliation'.[21] He was puzzled and wrote to Richard Shackleton: 'I do not know how to wish success to those whose Victory is to separate from us a large and noble part of our Empire. Still less do I wish success to injustice, oppression and absurdity.'[22] Burke did not expect the Americans to resist the British armies for long. In the interim, he feared the destruction of the system of government which had existed since the Glorious Revolution. He feared that 'other maxims of government and other grounds of obedience than those which have prevailed at and since the Glorious Revolution' were being propagated among the people.[23] By 1777 he was already convinced that the liberties of the country were in great danger. Burke believed that the imperial parliament had become a 'fund of despotism through which prerogative is extended by occasional powers, whenever an arbitrary will finds itself straitened by the restrictions of law'.[24] As late as 1777 in his Letter to the Sheriffs of Bristol Burke continued to cling to the pious hope that an acknowledged but unexercised right of taxation might satisfy the colonists. Clearly however, this was no longer possible and, in his heart, Burke knew it. In the 'Letter' he asserted that for parliament to concede American independence peacefully would damage the constitution less

---

[20] *Works*, III, 59.
[21] Burke to Charles O'Hara, 28 May 1775, *Correspondence*, III, 160–2.
[22] Burke to Richard Shackleton, 11 August 1776, ibid., 286–7.
[23] *Works*, IX, 193 (Address to the King, 1777).
[24] Ibid.

than would a war.[25] Thereafter Burke's advocacy of peace was closely connected to his support of American independence. Any hesitation Burke may have felt in supporting the Americans was dissipated when one of the British armies in America was defeated at Saratoga at the end of 1777. The struggle for the British constitution was being waged on the fields of America. Burke had not given up hope that the Americans might be tempted to return to the imperial fold. But he was no longer concerned to preserve imperial unity for its own sake. For Burke, the imperial conflict had become a struggle for liberty.

Burke believed passionately that the cause of liberty throughout the empire was at stake in the War of American Independence. If the Americans were to be defeated then the principles of Whiggism, those of the British constitution itself, would be overthrown. Liberty throughout the empire was indivisible. If it died in America it would not be long before it would be extinguished in Britain: 'you cannot have different rights and a different security in different parts of your dominions'.[26] Not only was the cause of liberty at stake on the battlefields of America, it was directly threatened at home by the war itself. Like many of his contemporaries opposed to the war, Burke clung to the double fear that if the British armies were victorious they might proceed to turn upon those who had opposed the war but that even if they were unsuccessful the military burdens under which the country was groaning would cause permanent damage to the body politic. The large number of military, naval and supply offices which had sprung up during the war was, for Burke, merely another example of the rising influence of the crown. Even when allowance has been made for rhetorical exaggeration, there can be little doubt that Burke was deeply afraid that the liberties of the empire would be cut off at their source and that there existed a threat to liberty in Britain greater in the 1770s than at any other time since the Glorious Revolution: 'Liberty is in danger of being made unpopular to Englishmen', he said. It was easy for Burke, in this vein, to interpret the coercive acts of 1774 as the symptoms of a new and sinister Toryism. He dismissed them as an attempt 'to dispose of the property of a whole people without their consent'.[27] Thus the suspension of Habeas Corpus appeared less as the erratic and ill judged response of a weak ministry to a crisis than as part of a deep laid plan. In short, the whole American crisis seemed to Burke to be reinforcing and strengthening the court system which had already been the object of his denunciation:

[25] *Works*, III, 147–54 (Letter to the Sheriffs).
[26] Ibid., IX, 194 (Address to the King). [27] Ibid., 176 (Letter to the Sheriffs).

War suspends the rules of moral obligation, and what is long suspended is in danger of being totally abrogated. Civil wars strike deepest of all into the manners of the people. They vitiate their politics; they corrupt their morals; they pervert even the natural taste and relish of equity and justice.[28]

Burke hated the war not merely because it threatened to extinguish liberty in the empire. He was alarmed at the Franco-American treaty of 1778. In the event of an American defeat, the French would be gravely weakened in Europe. Nothing could then stop the power of the crown from rising to uncontrollable proportions. On the other hand, if the Americans were victorious over the British then the power of France would be unrivalled in Europe, and then British security would be endangered, as happened in 1778 when a French invasion was nearly launched against British shores. National security and independence, as well as liberty, then, were threatened by the War of American Independence, a further substantial reason why Burke constantly championed the cause of peace and reconciliation.

Burke's American thought was thus less an imperial theory than a renewed plea for party. The Rockingham Whigs thought they were fighting not only the war but the court cabal as well. After the failure of their exertions to avert the war, many members of the party seceded from parliament in the winter of 1776–7. Rockingham wanted the 'infinite Comfort of not feeling – self accused – as having *ever abetted* the System in this Reign, which have brought on all the External Calamities, and which perhaps too, have laid the Foundations for endangering the Internal Felicities of the Constitution of this Country'.[29] Party had once more become a term of public abuse, associated as it was, with opposition to the war. Burke gloried in the controversy, 'For this rule of conduct I may be called in reproach a *party man*; but I am little affected with such aspersions. In the way which they call party, I worship the constitution of your fathers; and I shall never blush for my political company.'[30] Thus in opposing the ministry of Lord North over the American war, in using the kind of political language and in adopting the concepts that he did Burke was effectively extending his earlier political theory and applying it to imperial problems.

In his American attitudes, therefore, Burke was more of a party politician than a philosopher. Mistrusting philosophical speculation he

[28] *Works*, III, 152 (Letter to the Sheriffs).
[29] Rockingham to an unidentified recipient, early December 1776, Rockingham Papers, RI-1095a, Sheffield Public Library.
[30] *Works*, III, 197 (Letter to the Sheriffs).

did not think that political theory could resolve problems of imperial government. He asserted that:

> In the comprehensive dominion which the Divine Providence had put into our hands, instead of troubling our understandings with speculations concerning the unity of empire, and the identity of distinction of legislative powers, and inflaming our passions with the heat and pride of controversy, it was our duty, in all soberness, to conform our government to the character and circumstances of the several people who composed this mighty and strangely diversified mass.[31]

Such bluff Johnsonian common sense, such anti-philosophical philosophy, concealed, in fact, the extent to which Burke's American thinking rested upon three distinct yet related concepts. These were history, expediency and environment.

The lessons of history were never far from Burke's mind. He deplored the fact that ministers ignored history and introduced novel imperial practices which threatened popular liberties. He advocated an attitude towards the Americans consonant with 'the ancient policy and practice of the empire'[32] to which the Americans had lent their agreement. 'Recover your old ground, and your old tranquility' he told the Commons[33] and he went on to warn them:

> Be content to bind America by Laws of trade, you have always done it. Let this be your reason for binding their trade. Do not burthen them by taxes; you were not used to do so from the beginning. Let this be your reason for not taxing.[34]

Burke frequently comes close to asserting that political actions were justified, and only justified, if historical precedents existed for them. There is no doubt that he was just as historically minded in his imperial as in his domestic concerns. He sought to restore old practices. With his party, he looked into the past for his inspiration and for his principles. The past was a storehouse of practical wisdom of ever-present relevance. For example, to revive old practices would win the loyalty of the Americans. To innovate further would serve to alienate them even more. For Burke did not believe that there was anything radically wrong with the political or economic organization of the empire. For example, the colonists derived undeniable benefits from them because 'Their monopolist happened to be one of the richest men in the world' and thus they profited from British capital.[35] But, in Burke's view,

[31] *Works*, III, 182.   [32] Ibid., II, 430 (Speech on American Taxation).
[33] Ibid., 431.   [34] Ibid., 433.   [35] Ibid., 384.

in the 1760s parliament began to heap novel and crippling economic restrictions upon America for penny-pinching reasons. The economic policy of the Grenville and Chatham and North administrations struck at the very heart of the principle of 'no taxation without representation'. Burke placed his political opinions in a historical framework. Indeed his imperial attitudes are nothing less than a well-meaning endeavour to restore an imperial world which Burke fondly imagined to have existed in the good old days, before the court system corrupted and distorted political relationships of all kinds.

Closely connected with Burke's view of history was his concept of expedience. This operated at different levels of intellectual sophistication. Perhaps the most subtle of these was Burke's awareness of the uniqueness of historical situations, their complexity, their internal interconnections and external ramifications. Politics ought to take fully into account the peculiar idiosyncrasies of every historical artefact. But such a mentality bred a thorough timidity of undertaking drastic action. He was instinctively fond of supporting established institutions and rights established by history and by custom. Not for Burke the lavish gestures and the large-scale reforms. It was enough to preserve the heritage of the past. This was, in fact, the best means of planning for the future. He asserted that the repeal of the Stamp Act and the Declaratory Act had been decided,

> on principles, not of constitutional right, but on those of expedience, of equity, of lenity and of the true interests present and future of that great object for which alone the colonies were founded, navigation and commerce.[36]

Right political judgement must always relate to the practical rather than the theoretical features of the case, and, in particular, take note of the interests of men and institutions. But Burke's notion of expedience operated at the political level too. He was fond of making the distinction between a right and its enforcement. He insisted not only that the military enforcement of a right was liable to lead to evil consequences but that 'we have no sort of *experience* in favour of force as an instrument in the rule of our colonies'.[37] It was thus unprecedented and did not enjoy the presumption of history.

The extent to which Burke related expedience and history will already be apparent, yet his awareness of the importance of environmental issues throws both into relief. Burke strongly reinforced his argument against the use of force by his discussion of the nature of

[36] *Works*, II, 168–9 (*Observations on a . . . State of the Nation*).
[37] Ibid., III, 48 (Speech on Conciliation).

American society and the factors which conditioned the spirit of its people. Burke took account of the rising population in the colonies, the booming commerce and the thriving agriculture. Such considerations ruled out what Burke described as a 'partial, narrow, contracted, pinched, occasional system for dealing with America'.[38] Burke displayed considerable insight into the spirit of the American people and the conditions which had formed it including traditions of protestantism, free thought, free education and self-government. His understanding of the critically important relationship between circumstances and policy was to be a common element in his political philosophy. But it does not appear to have occurred to Burke that the old mercantilist framework of empire was no longer sufficient to contain these dynamic social forces. Although he was able to utilize his familiarity with American history and society to demonstrate the irrelevance of a military solution to the colonial question, he was unable to advance a more realistic solution himself. Even if it had been possible to restore the imperial situation which existed before 1763, it is extremely doubtful if the Americans would have been satisfied. Burke was willing to go to almost any lengths to restore the old empire. Indeed, he was willing to go so far that he stumbled almost by accident, upon a new concept of the empire.

Burke always maintained that the imperial sovereignty of Britain should be recognized by the colonists, otherwise 'the presiding authority of Great Britain as the head, the arbiter, and director of the whole empire, would vanish into an empty name, without operation or energy'.[39] Nevertheless, he was loath to advocate measures to enforce the supremacy of the imperial government:

> The very idea of subordination of parts, excludes this notion of simple and undivided unity. England is the head; but she is not the head and members too. Ireland has ever had from the beginning a separate, but not an independent, legislature; which far from distracting, promoted the union of whole.[40]

For Burke the empire was a collection of diverse political units under the general and paternal supremacy of the mother parliament. He went, perhaps, as far as anyone could, towards reconciling local separation with imperial unity given the limitations of contemporary thinking about the imperial question, especially the preoccupation with rights. Burke summarized his ideal of the empire thus:

> We have a great empire to rule, composed of a vast mass of hetero-

[38] *Works*, III, 36.   [39] Ibid., II, 169–70 (*Observations*).   [40] Ibid., 113.

geneous governments, all more or less free and popular in their forms, all to be kept in peace, and kept out of conspiracy with one another, all to be kept in subordination to this country; while the spirit of an extensive and intricate and trading interest pervades the whole, always qualifying and often controlling, every general idea of constitution or government. It is a great and difficult object; and I wish we may possess wisdom and temper enough to manage it as we ought. Its importance is infinite.[41]

The role of parliament in the empire was two-fold. The first arose from its function as the local legislature of Great Britain itself

The other, and I think her nobler capacity, is what I call her *imperial character*; in which, as from the throne of heaven, she superintends all the several inferior legislatures, and guides and controls them all, without annihilating any. As all these provincial legislatures are only co-ordinate to each other, they ought to be subordinate to her, else they can neither preserve mutual peace, nor hope for mutual justice, nor effectually afford mutual assistance.[42]

Burke considered that the provincial legislatures should be independent of the mother parliament unless they proved themselves unequal 'to the common ends of their institution'.[43] Parliament must therefore supply these occasional deficiencies from her boundless reserve of sovereignty. Burke well understood that the spheres of authority of the central and local legislatures were difficult to define but he assumed that wise policy operating in accordance with circumstances would establish a viable relationship between mother country and colony. Burke was fond of observing that the real cement of empire was not the laws, still less was it physical coercion or economic subordination: it was more subtle but far more powerful. We quote again Burke's apparent anticipation of the ideal of the modern commonwealth:

My hold of the colonies is in the close affection which grows from common names, from kindred blood, from similar priveleges, and equal protection. These are ties, which, though light as air, are as strong as links of iron. Let the colonies always keep the idea of their civil rights associated with your government; they will cling and grapple to you; and no force under heaven will be of power to tear them from their allegiance. But let it be once understood, that your government may be one thing, and their privileges another; that these two things may exist without any mutual relation; the

[41] *Works*, II, 167.   [42] Ibid., II, 436 (Speech on American Taxation).
[43] Ibid.

cement is gone; the cohesion is loosened; and everything hastens to decay and dissolution.

As he put it 'Magnanimity in politics is not seldom the truest wisdom; and a great empire and little minds go ill together.'[44]

Burke's American thought was the series of public utterances of a party politician, a collection of speeches and addresses and plans whose purpose it was to cope with urgent problems. He viewed the American problem through the eyes of a British parliamentarian – indeed, he could do no other – and although he came nearer than many of his contemporaries to understanding the problem of empire, he could not separate in his own mind the threat to American liberties posed by parliamentary taxation from the threat to the British constitution posed by the court system. This is the essential link between Burke's domestic and imperial thinking. The fact that parliament acquiesced in the taxation of Americans lent a conspiratorial air to the imperial question, in which the sinister cabal around George III was equally intent upon destroying the liberties of Americans as of Englishmen. Burke's imperial thinking embraced the ideal of returning to a 'golden age' of imperial relationships; this ideal of restoring a former age rather than anticipating a new one, characterized Burke's imperial as well as his domestic thought. In the same way that Burke was not and could not be the prophet of the two party system, or the modern system of responsible government, so he cannot be truly described as the prophet of the modern commonwealth of nations.

[44] *Works*, II, III, 126 (Speech on Conciliation).

Chapter IV

The Imperial Problem: Ireland

We saw in our examination of Burke's American thought that his ideas were called forth by political circumstances over which he had no control. The second of the imperial questions with which he had to deal – that of Ireland – was more complex than that of America. It was, in fact, much more than an imperial situation. Social and economic realities lay at the root of the problem. The mass of the native peasantry were Catholic. They resented restrictions placed both upon their religion and their political activities by the Protestant minority, many of them absentee English landlords, who ruled the country and its people. Catholics had no prospect of acquiring education or political power. They had neither the vote nor the right to sit in parliament. The Irish parliament at Dublin had little independent authority and tamely followed the policy of the imperial legislature. The government of Ireland was in the hands of the Lord-Lieutenant who was appointed by the British government. The parliament of Ireland was managed by undertakers who wielded a pro-English majority. In short, a corrupt minority exercised a Protestant Ascendancy over the country. After 1760 the native Irish slowly began to stir and to manifest their discontent with the situation. They came up against the power not only of the Protestant Ascendancy but also that of the British government. For long the Ascendancy and the imperial authorities had presented a united front to the Catholic Irish but conflict between them gradually came to the surface. In this political minefield Burke had to tread with care.

Burke, of course, was an Irishman and his solicitousness for his native country was one of the motivating aspects of his early thought. He admitted in 1780 that it had always been one of his political aims 'to be somewhat useful to the place of my Birth and education'[1] and to

[1] For his detailed vindication of his conduct with respect to Ireland in 1778

attempt to manifest what he described as 'an utter abhorrence of all kinds of public injustice and oppression' which led him, as he said, to take up the crusade of Ireland.[2] He was pleased to go with Hamilton to Ireland in the early 1760's but he was undoubtedly moved by the wretched condition of his fellow countrymen, and nauseated by the horrible violence with which the agrarian disturbances (attributed to the so-called Whiteboys) of these years were put down.

It was about this time that Burke wrote his *Tracts on the Popery Laws*, from which much of our knowledge of his early Irish attitudes can be gleaned. The *Tracts* were a polemic against the injustice and inhumanity of the penal laws against the Irish Catholics, laws which appeared to Burke to aim at the destruction of Catholic property and weaken the institution of Catholic marriage and promote the division of Ireland into two hostile groups. Yet, although the language of the *Tracts* was extravagant their substance was less extreme. He demanded better treatment for the Catholics but neither the dissolution of the Protestant establishment nor any substantial change in the structure of Irish society. Even when he was most radical Burke remained profoundly conservative by temperament and inclination.

Burke's first public stand on Irish questions as a party politican was made in opposition – pretty factious opposition, at that – to a ministerial proposal in 1773 to lay a tax upon the property of absentee Irish landowners. Now Burke, in his nationalistic youth, had advocated just such a tax but he found political objections to it in 1773. Not only was Lord Rockingham one of the greatest of the absentee landlords but many others in the party held land in Ireland too. Burke, then, had to toe the party line and join in the party's opposition to the tax. He proclaimed that if the tax passed then many of the absentees would be forced by economic reasons to take up residence in Ireland. Burke sincerely believed that if they did so the natural bonds between England and Ireland would be weakened and the fabric of the empire loosened. But Burke knew as well as anyone how much harm the absentee landlords did Ireland. His blind obedience to the party line over this matter does his reputation little credit. In view of the lifetime of devoted service which he gave to his country his attitude requires explanation. What may be said in his defence is that Irish affairs were still relatively peaceful and that the world situation had not invested her with the critically important geographical and strategic role which she acquired later in the decade. And furthermore there was nothing

and 1779, see his letter to Thomas Burgh, dated 1 January 1780, printed in *The Works of Edmund Burke* (2 vols 1834), II, 407–14.

[2] Burke to J. Curry, 14 August 1779, *Correspondence*, IV, 118–20.

inconsistent in Burke, the protagonist of the Declaratory Act, defending the powers of the imperial parliament against a narrowly nationalistic bill.

Burke was an Irish patriot, but, more than that, he was an imperialist. When the American War of Independence had broken out, Ireland could have taken advantage of England's embarrassments to seek local advantage. Burke took a wider view, however, asserting the identity of interests between the two countries within the empire. He saw the importance of Ireland's geographical position in relation to France and England. To keep Ireland in safe hands, Burke saw that the Irish must be made happy, their connection with Britain entirely voluntary. As the crisis of the empire developed in the late 1770s Burke saw the Irish problem in an imperial framework. Indeed, he was convinced that Ireland had an important part to play in the current crisis. 'Ireland was never in the situation of real honour and real consequence in which she now stands. She has the Ballance of the Empire and perhaps its fate for ever, in her hands.' What Burke wanted was for the Irish parliament to address both the king and the English parliament against pursuing a coercive policy in America. If it did 'It was impossible that they should not succeed.'[3] Burke was wrong. It was, in fact, not only possible, but perhaps inevitable! No such address was forthcoming. Burke complained 'Ireland has missed the most glorious opportunity ever indulged by heaven to a subordinate State, that of being the safe and certain mediatour in the quarrels of a great Empire'.[4] What worried Burke and many of his contemporaries was that Ireland, far from being impartial in the struggle between Britain and her colonies, might try to emulate the Americans. This was something against which Burke constantly struggled by seeking to improve the domestic situation of the Irish themselves.

Burke had no illusions about his native land. He knew that its political system was rotten, that the mass of the Catholic peasantry were unwilling to take part in constructive political action and that the ruling Protestants, including both the landed and the monied interests, were unwilling for selfish reasons to assist England in her struggle against the Americans.[5] Burke was right to have reservations about his fellow countrymen. The American Revolution, and especially the Declaration of Independence, had made an impact upon Ireland, where the ruling class – but especially the Presbyterians – began to demand a greater measure of independence of the mother country, a

[3] Burke to Richmond, 26 September, 1775, *Correspondence*, III, 217–20.
[4] Burke to Lord Charlemont, 4 June 1776, ibid., 270–1.
[5] Burke to Charles James Fox, 8 October 1777, ibid., 380–8.

demand which England was hardly in a position to refuse especially when the Irish leaders began to acquire popular support for their attempts to widen the sphere of toleration for Roman Catholics.

Considering both the seriousness of the Irish situation and the degree of Burke's concern for his country, he was surprisingly slow to take any initiative on this topic. He supported silently a measure proposed by one of the most independent and talented men of his party, Sir George Savile, to extend toleration for English Catholics. This passed in 1778 and allowed them to lease and sell land. This was merely a prelude to a similar measure for Ireland. Burke now took it upon himself to advise the Irish Catholics to remain loyal to the throne and to petition peacefully for some relaxation of the penal laws which he had condemned in the *Tracts* a decade and a half earlier.[6] Burke believed that religious and civil toleration must proceed together. One was useless without the other. He even opposed a relief bill in 1782 because it excluded Catholics from the franchise and from holding offices. For Burke, the price of religious toleration should not be civil slavery. Civil freedom should precede religious toleration and provide a foundation for its development. Burke had, therefore, a secular view of toleration. He viewed it as a civic as much as a religious question. Thus, in his view, the act of 1782, extended religious toleration 'but it puts a new bolt on civil rights, and rivets it to the old one'.[7]

Toleration was, perhaps, less important an issue in Irish politics in the age of the American Revolution than the commercial relationship of the mother-country with its dependency. Burke believed that some easing of Ireland's restrictive trade laws was urgent, especially when the American war began to cause serious dislocations in Irish trade. Burke clung courageously to his opinions, even at the cost of alienating his Bristol constituents, who bitterly recognized that they would be among the first victims of Burke's generosity towards the Irish.

Burke's courage and selflessness in advocating far-reaching changes in the economic structure of the empire are however less interesting than the arguments he used to support his proposal. Yet again he rested his case upon an appeal to history, arguing that his proposals merely restored the economic arrangements of the empire to what they had been in the later seventeenth century. The Navigation Act of 1672

---

[6] Burke to J. Perry, 12 July 1778, ibid., IV, 5–10. For details of these proceedings see A. P. Levack, 'Edmund Burke, his Friends and the Dawn of Irish Catholic Emancipation', *Catholic Historical Review*, XXXVII (1951); T. H. D. Mahoney, 'Edmund Burke and Rome', ibid., XL (1953). Professor Mahoney's *Edmund Burke and Ireland* (Harvard University Press, 1960) is the most detailed and authoritative account of its subject.

[7] Burke to Lord Kenmare, 21 February 1782, *Correspondence*, IV, 405–18.

and its benefits applied to Ireland as well as to England.[8] It was only
since the Williamite oppression that Ireland had lost her commercial
freedom. History and justice were thus both on the side of the Irish.
Ireland had demonstrated her loyalty to England on several occasions
and furnished her with troops. It was in Britain's own interest, therefore, to reward such fidelity at least with an opportunity for the Irish
to compete equally with the English on the home market. Burke was
also conscious of another, more ominous, argument that the Irish
would force the English to grant such a concession unless it were
granted voluntarily.[9] For Burke, the interests of Bristol, the interests
of England and of Ireland were subordinate to the interests of the
empire as a whole. He regarded himself not merely as a member of
parliament but also as a member of an imperial parliament. Only by
adopting an imperial attitude could Ireland be saved from going the
way of America.[10]

Events completely justified the wisdom of Burke's magnanimity.
1779 was remarkable in Ireland for the sudden growth of the Volunteer
Movement. The Volunteers were a body of militia. They had sprung
up as a defensive reaction against the incursions of American privateers.
They could easily be directed, however, against the British and used
to extract concessions from the North administration. The Volunteers
were contemptuous of the scanty religious and commercial concessions
which the British government was offering in 1779. As the year wore
on, Catholics were admitted into the Volunteers and by the autumn
of 1779 Ireland seemed poised to go the way of America. Not only
was the Irish parliament demanding freer trade. Forty thousand
Volunteers pressed home its demand. The American pattern was
clearly being repeated when, in the autumn of 1779, non-importation
agreements levelled against English goods proliferated in Ireland.
Burke of course was deeply alarmed by these symptoms of an impending
Irish separatism. He was a British imperialist before he was an Irish
nationalist. He approved warmly therefore of the measures that North

[8] The Rockingham–Shelburne ministry was agreed on few things. A solution
to the Irish problem, however, was one of them. The ministry repealed an act
of 1719 which applied the legislation of the English parliament directly and
automatically to Ireland. Other detailed measures passed by the ministry
limited the authority of the British Privy Council to amend Irish laws.

[9] See Burke's speech of 5 May 1778, *The Parliamentary History*, XIX,
1119–24. It is Burke's Letter to Sir Hercules Langrishe (1792) which contains
his most detailed discussion of the Glorious Revolution and its effects upon
Ireland, *Works*, VI, 334–6.

[10] See Burke's speech of 15 February 1779, *The Parliamentary History*, XX,
133.

rushed through parliament at the turn of the year.[11] Burke supported free trade in the empire not only because it would be beneficial to the whole empire, not just because it would benefit Ireland but also because it was clearly in the interests of the mother country herself to relax her mercantilist stranglehold upon Ireland.[12] Burke was, therefore, just as uninterested in the traditional *rights* of the British parliament over Ireland as he was in its *rights* over America. He believed that inequalities and grievances ought to be redressed irrespective of rights. Events were soon to demonstrate how wise Burke's indifference to legislative sovereignty really was. 'Our late misfortunes have taught us the danger and mischief of a restrictive coercive and partial policy.' He had believed for some time that 'The prosperity, arising from an enlarged and liberal system improved all its objects and the participation of a trade with flourishing countries is much better than the monopoly of want and penury.'[13] And he ridiculed the prospect that 'America was to be conquered, in order that Ireland should *not* trade thither; whilst the miserable Trade, which she is permitted to carry on to other places, has been torn to pieces in the struggle'. He did not believe trade between England and Ireland was limited, 'as if the objects of mutual demand and consumption, could not stretch beyond the bounds of our Jealousies'.[14] One other argument in favour of free trade appealed to him. It would further the prosperity of the urban middle class (among which was numbered a small but significant Catholic minority) and weaken the power of the Protestant Ascendancy.

The next objective of the Irish was to prevent the British government from retracting the commercial concessions which it had so reluctantly granted. This could only be attained by the Irish being granted some measure of legislative independence. In 1780 and 1781 this prospect became increasingly attractive to the Irish; after Britain's defeat by the Americans at Yorktown towards the end of 1781 it became irresistible. The Rockingham – Shelburne ministry of 1782 which succeeded the ministry of North could do no other than grant legislative independence to Ireland. By this time, indeed, the Volunteers and the 'Patriot' party led by Ireland's liberal statesman, Henry Grattan[15]

[11] These included the removal of restrictions upon the import of Irish wool and glass into England and the opening to the Irish of markets in America, the West Indies and Africa.

[12] Burke to T. Burgh, 1 January 1780, loc. cit.

[13] Burke to Samuel Span, 9 April 1778, *Correspondence*, III, 426.

[14] Burke to Hartford, Cowles & Co., 2 May 1778, ibid., 440–1.

[15] The greatest Irish politician of his generation and the architect of Irish legislative independence. Indeed, in Irish history, the Irish assembly of 1782–1801 is referred to as 'Grattan's Parliament'. .

had become the allies of the Rockingham Whigs and the counter-weights to the Protestant Ascendancy. Burke took little active part in Irish affairs, excluded as he was from cabinet discussions. Not that he was uninterested. He went clean against the wishes of his party colleagues in criticizing the grant of legislative independence. Burke's disapproval was founded upon his fear that it tended towards the complete separation of Ireland from the mother country and the disintegration of the empire. Legislative independence would undermine the position of the Lord Lieutenant and weaken the position of the Irish Catholics. (The imperial parliament had always existed as a final court of appeal for them but after 1782 it would no longer be able to inquire into the actions of the Protestant Ascendancy.) Another aspect of Burke's imperial conservatism becomes evident. Burke wished to maintain the traditional structure of the empire by restoring traditional usages in each constituent part, and with traditional usages, traditional loyalties.

In an attempt to establish greater security for the Irish Catholics, however, Burke now reversed his earlier position and conceded the right of Catholics to hold office. This reversal of his earlier attitude also contradicts his attitude towards the English Dissenters but it followed logically enough from the new situation in which Irish Catholics found themselves after 1782. Those Catholics who managed to attain office would be able to some extent to protect those who did not. As usual, this was a political rather than a philosophical reason; for Burke's attitude to Irish legislative independence anticipated his controversial opposition to Pitt's proposals of 1785 for free trade with Ireland. No doubt Burke followed his party in its factious opposition to Pitt's scheme.[16] No doubt, too, his wish to acquire popularity in Ireland played some part in persuading him to resist the proposals. Yet his fear that Pitt's proposals might lead in time to the economic separation of Ireland from England was, at least, consistent with his earlier and frequently expressed concern to maintain the integrity of the empire.

The French Revolution caused further changes in Burke's developing and sometimes complex attitude towards Ireland. The origin of Burke's new concern was his fear that the depressed Catholic peasantry might attempt to emulate the French, to destroy the Protestant Ascendancy and establish a Jacobin revolutionary power, allied to France, in Ireland. In the last years of his life, therefore, Burke toiled increasingly

[16] Pitt wished to promote the commercial prosperity of Ireland in an attempt to lower the political tension. This he proposed to do by liberalizing trade between the two countries.

to safeguard Ireland from revolution. Towards this end he lent his aid to the powerful Catholic Association, tried to restrain it from violence and excesses and encouraged it to aim for the amelioration of the lot of the Catholics and a complete revision of the penal laws. He supported its attempts to admit Catholics into the professions, into the magistracy and to the franchise.[17] In his attempts to safeguard the unity of the empire and to maintain the loyalty of the Catholic population of Ireland, Burke was forced into a thoroughgoing re-examination of his earlier ideas. He continued to work, but now with renewed vigour, for the repeal of the penal laws. Reflecting his attitude towards America in the 1770s (when he had scorned the idea of indicting a whole people) Burke reasserted his belief that the penal laws formed no part of the ancient constitution of the empire and that if Ireland were to be kept within the folds of the empire they must be done away with. This attitude was typical of Burke, both in his concern for the integrity of the empire and his concern for popular liberties. Yet surely Burke was guilty of inconsistency in at least one part of his proposed treatment of the Irish Catholics: his willingness to admit them to the franchise when he was so vehemently opposed to its extension in England.

For Burke, of course, the situation of the two countries was different. In Ireland the Catholics had no representation at all. They were not even 'virtually' represented in the Irish parliament whose representative character had been strangled by the Ascendancy. Therefore, even if the result of admitting the Catholics to the franchise were the increased corruption which Burke anticipated he nevertheless thought it a price worth paying for keeping Ireland in the British empire. There was a further argument in favour of parliamentary reform in Ireland. It might save the country from an Irish Catholic revolution. Burke opposed violent revolution in Ireland for many reasons. Fundamentally, he could not see that violence was necessary when political channels for reform still remained open. Burke did not believe that the British constitution established between 1688 and 1714 forbade Catholic enfranchisement; to enfranchise them, therefore, would not be a violation of the constitution, rather the contrary.

As every one knows, that a great part of the Constitution of the Irish House of Commons was founded about the year 1614, expressly

[17] Edmund sent his son, Richard to Ireland in 1792 to act as the agent of the Catholic Association in an attempt to reform the administration of that country. In this he was unsuccessful. In the following year, after the outbreak of war between England and France, Pitt relented and extended the vote to the Irish Catholics upon the same basis as that already enjoyed by the Protestants.

for bringing that House into a state of dependance, and that the new Representative was at that time seated and installed by force and violence, nothing can be more impolitic than for those who wish the House to stand on its present basis, (as for one I most sincerely do) to make it appear to have kept too much the principle of its first institution, and to continue to be as little a virtual, as it is an actual representative of the Commons. It is the degeneracy of such an institution so vicious in its principle, that is to be wished for. If Men have the real Benefit of a Sympathetic Representation, none but those who are heated and intoxicated with Theory will look for any other. This sort of Representation, my dear Sir, must wholly depend not on the force with which it is upheld, but upon the prudence of those who have influence upon it. Indeed without some such prudence in the use of Authority, I do not know, at least in the present time, how any power can long continue.[18]

Burke did not believe that a Catholic franchise would amount to anything like an attack upon property by numbers. Since 1778 the Catholics had enjoyed the right to acquire property. They had thus acquired an interest to uphold and defend. They, or at least the propertied Catholics, deserved the vote. Burke, then, in admitting Catholics to the vote was extending, not contradicting his own principles. Finally, we may note that Burke never stated that the franchise was a right. Its extension was a matter of expediency. The danger that numbers would be set against property would be reduced by admitting 'settled, permanent substance in lieu of the numbers'.[19] Thus Burke strengthened property against numbers. After a century of discrimination it was a matter of urgent necessity for the British government to conciliate the Irish Catholics. Burke well knew that to enfranchise Catholic property would only affect the outcome of a handful of elections. He wanted not electoral change but a symbolic public act to win the trust of the Catholics. And, in any case, the enfranchisement of the Catholics said Burke was 'not an innovation in the constitution but a restoration of it, the removal of an innovation'.[20]

Yet the swirling and dangerous cross currents of the Irish problem led Burke to discard some of his optimistic ideas. By the end of 1792 the Irish situation was seriously and rapidly deteriorating. The hitherto moderate Catholic Association had fallen into the hands of Wolf Tone,

[18] Burke to an unidentified recipient, February 1797, *Correspondence*, IX, 253–63.
[19] *Works*, VI, 311, 368–73 (Letter to Langrishe, 1792).
[20] Speech on the Address to the Throne, 13 December 1792, *Speeches*, IV, 80.

who supported and propagated the principles of the French Revolution. The outbreak of war between France and Britain in February 1793 ignited a critical situation. At once, the British government adopted the policy of relief which Burke had been advocating for some time. The Relief Act of 1793 admitted the Irish Catholics to both the parliamentary and to the municipal franchises, to the magistracy, and allowed them to sit on juries and to hold commissions. These substantial concessions did not effectively quieten the Irish scene. The tide of revolutionary enthusiasm rose so high that Burke became thoroughly alarmed. He proclaimed that all men whatever their politics or religion must unite against the atheistic anarchy of Jacobinism. In the way of achieving this national inter-denominational crusade against Jacobinism, however, stood the almost insuperable obstacle of the Protestant Ascendancy.

Burke had always hated the Ascendancy. He regarded it as a selfish and sectional attempt by a part only of the Protestants to arrogate to themselves exclusively the privileges of citizenship. They perpetuated their oligarchic dominion by wholesale bribery and corruption. The envy, jealousy and suspicion which resulted were fatal to Burke's hope for national unity in the 1790s. The Relief Act of 1793 had not weakened the power of the Ascendancy: rather it had served to entrench it more strongly.

> That the late change in the Laws has not made any alteration in their Tempers; except that of aggravating their habitual pride by resentment and vexation. They have resolved, to make one, among the many unhappy discoveries of our times. It is this; that neither the Laws, nor the dispositions of the chief executive Magistrate are able to give security to the people, whenever certain leading men in the Country, and in office are against them. They have actually made the discovery; and a dreadful one it is, for Kings, Laws and Subjects: This is what makes all Ideas of Ascendancy in particular factions, whether distinguished by party names taken from Theology or from Politicks so mischievous as they have been. Wherever such Factions, predominate in such a manner, that they come to link (which without loss of time they are sure to do) a pecuniary and personal Interest with the licentiousness of a party domination, nothing can secure those that are under it. If this was not clear enough, upon a consideration of the nature of things, and the nature of Man, the late proceedings in Ireland, subsequent to the repeal of the penal laws would leave no doubt of it.[21]

[21] Burke to Thomas Hussey, 4 February 1795, *Correspondence*, VIII, 138.

It should not be thought that Burke was encouraging an attack upon the Irish aristocracy. Rather he was trying to establish one. As early as 1792 he had proclaimed that he would like to replace the Ascendancy by 'an aristocratick interest . . . an interest of property and education . . . and to strengthen by every prudent means, the authority and influence of men of that description.'[22] He was not thus arguing for a more democratic form of government but for a more aristocratic one, 'provided that the personal authority of individual nobles be kept in due bounds, that their cabals and factions are guarded against with a severe vigilance'.[23] There is some danger that we may mistake and misunderstand Burke's ultimate objectives in Ireland. His sense of nationalism, his conception of the role of Ireland in the empire, his wish to extend toleration and civic rights to the Catholics and, most of all, his passionate desire to break the power of the Ascendancy— tend to conceal the fact that he wished, after all, to establish a society in Ireland dominated by the aristocracy, not by the Ascendancy of the Protestants. Government, for Burke, ought to be aristocratic: 'Our constitution is not made for great, general, and prescriptive exclusions, sooner or later it will destroy them, or they will destroy the constitution.'[24] The purpose of politics was to promote reconciliation. A 'prudent and enlarged' policy ought to be pursued by governments, especially the imperial government in Ireland in the 1790s. If they did not then it would be all too easy for the Jacobins to promote attacks upon religion, property, and 'old traditionary institutions.'[25]

Burke, therefore, opposed the persecution of the Catholics because the stability of Irish society was at stake, and, with it, the security of the empire. His hatred of persecution did not arise from a purely philosophical scruple but from the harsh realities of politics in the tempestuous decade of the 1790s. Besides, it was not so much the case that the persecution was wrong; it was futile. Two centuries of persecution had only strengthened the cohesion of the Catholics and their loyalty to their religion. Events in the last few years of Burke's life appeared to justify his humanitarianism. The British government ignored Burke's advice and relied increasingly upon the use of force and government by the Ascendancy to maintain its rule in Ireland. Although Burke did not live to see the rebellion of 1798, he lived long enough to deplore the growing extremism of the Catholics as well as the blind obduracy of the Protestants. At all costs he was determined to fight the forces of Irish nationalism. Any talk, or any hint, of Irish home rule horrified him:

[22] *Works*, VI, 344–5 (Letter to Sir Hercules Langrishe, 1792).
[23] Ibid., 304.   [24] Ibid.   [25] Ibid., 310.

For, in the name of God, what Grievance had Ireland, as Ireland, to complain of with regard to Great Britain? Unless the protection of the most powerful Country upon earth, giving all her privileges without exception in common to Ireland, and reserving to herself only the painful pre-eminence of tenfold Burthens to be a matter of complaint. The Subject, as a subject is as free in Ireland as he is in England—as a member of the Empire, an Irishman has every privilege of a natural born Englishman, in every part of it, in every occupation, and in every branch of Commerce.[26]

He wished, therefore, to maintain the imperial relationship for the sake of Ireland as much as for the sake of England. Lying beneath the varying and complex elements of Burke's Irish thought, therefore, can be discerned an imperial mentality which renders coherent the divergent aspects of his thinking and makes intelligible the fanatical tone of his later writings.

The sense of apocalyptic despair which Burke felt towards the end of his life over Irish affairs was far more than a senile dread of disorder. He feared the consequences of Irish independence: instant subjugation at the hands of the French. If England did not dominate Ireland then France surely would. 'Ireland *constitutionally* is independent – *Politically* she never can be so.'[27] France would destroy Catholicism and Protestantism as well; everything, therefore, must be subordinated to keeping Ireland free of French influences. In particular, Ireland must be saved from the naivete of her Jacobin sons who fondly believed that the only way to save themselves from the Ascendancy was to go the way of the French.[28] At the same time, he thoroughly understood the almost universal hatred among Catholics for the Ascendancy. He well knew that further emancipation would not reconcile them to the empire. Nothing short of universal suffrage would satisfy them. But any concession would be regarded by the Catholics as a show of weakness.[29] Nevertheless, he was determined to save his country. In his last months Burke would have made any sacrifice, including the concession of universal suffrage, even the destruction of the Ascendancy, to conciliate the Catholics. He died on 9 July 1797 in the unhappy belief that the Ascendancy was hardening its grip on the country and that revolution was now inevitable.

It was well that he died before the rebellion of 1798 for that event

26 Burke to Thomas Hussey, 18 May 1795, *Correspondence*, VIII, 246–7.
27 Burke to an unidentified recipient, February 1797, loc. cit.
28 Burke to Thomas Hussey, 18 May 1795, loc. cit.
29 Burke to Lord Fitzwilliam, 7 May 1797, *Correspondence*, IX, 330–1.

marked the complete disappointment of his hopes. Like many of his contemporaries, Burke could scarcely keep pace with the rapid changes in the British empire in the later eighteenth century. Like many of his contemporaries, he failed to think out a satisfactory solution to the tragic Irish problem. Yet his Irish thought well illustrates the constant pragmatism and undogmatic realism which inform so much of his political philosophy. He did not attempt to force an interpretation of events into conformity with an arbitrary view of the empire. There is, however, a consistency in his overall view of Irish society and Irish history, which ensures that his flexibility does not become a superficial expediency. His humanitarianism, manifested in his anxiety to extend a greater degree of toleration to the Irish Catholics, shines through every aspect of his long career of concern for the Irish. His distaste for the corruption and exclusiveness of the Ascendancy was always with him. Finally, his conviction that the destiny of Ireland was indissolubly linked with that of England provided yet another plank of consistency in the history of his Irish thought. For here, as in his American thought, Burke was the great conciliator, trying to restore the imperial links between Irishmen and Englishmen on the one hand, and between Irishmen and Irishmen on the other.

Chapter V

The Imperial Problem: India

Burke's ideas on British rule in India were consistent in their general outline with other aspects of his imperial thinking. On America he had objected to parliament's *right* to tax the colonies arbitrarily. On Indian affairs he opposed the *right* of the East India Company to govern India arbitrarily. On neither issue did he deny the status of the legislative right involved. For Burke there existed profound humanitarian and moral issues which transcended legislative custom. Similarly, his later works attacked the French revolutionaries for destroying the *ancien régime* in France and in Europe. This attitude was consonant with his attacks upon the East India Company for its destruction of an *ancien régime* in India, for its tampering with chartered rights, for its destruction of an ancient ruling class. His solicitousness for the Irish Catholics was matched by his concern for the welfare of the mass of the Indian people. Further, the awareness of environmental and socializing factors which he had displayed on American affairs was reflected in a similar understanding of Indian society. In a debate in 1781 he asserted that 'we must now be guided, as we ought to have been with respect to India, by studying the genius, the temper, and the manner of the people, and adapting to them the laws that we establish'.[1] In this way, different aspects of Burke's thought complement each other, develop comparable themes and reflect similar attitudes. Burke was always ready to expand his vision and to incorporate into his thought new circumstances and new situations. This is one reason why his thought is not dull and uniform but vibrant and variable. Burke was not impressed by the 'right' of the East India Company to misgovern India. Such a right constituted a monopoly and therefore a trust, over which parliament should exercise vigilance. The Company's

[1] Speech of 27 June 1781, *The Parliamentary History*, XXII, 555.

rights were not unlimited. If it violated the trust which parliament reposed in it then parliament could and should revoke it. It was not to be, however, before the 1780s that he expounded fully his doctrine of the trust owed by the imperial parliament to the people of India. The company's 'right', therefore, was restricted by the necessity for it to govern in accordance with the habits of the people themselves, with their history and character, rather than in accordance with the paper precedents of legislative custom.

The nature of Burke's involvement in Indian politics can only be appreciated and its intensity understood by realizing how far he felt himself to be personally involved in the affairs of the company and of Warren Hastings. His crusades to reform the government of India coincided with the decline of Burke's party fervour, when his active and restless intellect was hungry for new challenges and starved of political idealism. His persecution of Hastings began during the dark days of Burke's career, when his public reputation was at its lowest and when he felt the need to justify his career to posterity. To this end, the impeachment of Hastings would be his monument.[2] He pored over partisan accounts of the Company's rule in India – and of Hastings' part in it – and read into them a conflict of principles, a conflict in which he, Burke, was on the side of right and Hastings the side of wrong. For Burke, the impeachment was to be like a medieval morality play, acted out in public, bristling with salutary moral and political lessons for Britain. There can be no disputing the fact that Burke considered his Indian activities to be the most important events of his career. Towards the end of his life he wrote:

> Let everything I have done, said or written be forgotten but this. I have struggled with the great and the little on this point during the greater part of my active Life; and I wish after death, to have my Defiance of the Judgements of those, who consider the dominion of the glorious Empire given by an incomprehensible dispensation of the Divine providence into our hands as nothing more than an opportunity of gratifying for the lowest of their purposes, the lowest of their passions and that for such poor rewards, and for the most part, indirect and silly Bribes, as indicate even more the folly than the corruption of these infamous and contemptible wretches.[3]

[2] Burke to Sir Philip Francis, 10 December 1785, *Correspondence*, V, 241–4. (Hastings had been Governor-General of Bengal between 1772 and 1785.)

[3] Burke to French Laurence, *circa* 27 February 1796, *Correspondence*, VIII, 397–9.

Burke was determined to refute the charge that he had been moved merely by personal antagonism against Warren Hastings.

> In reality, you know that I am no enthusiast, but (according to the powers that God has given me) a sober and reflecting man. I have not even the other very bad excuse, of acting from personal resentment, or from the sense of private injury – never having received any; nor can I plead ignorance, no man ever having taken more pains to be informed. Therefore, *I* say, Remember.[4]

It is important to understand how *symbolic* the impeachment was for Burke. He did not seriously expect to convict Hastings. What he aimed to do through the theatrical drama of the impeachment was to assert certain general principles which should be observed in the government of India. It is not too much to say that he was less concerned with the truth about Hastings' rule than with the morality of imperial responsibilities in the sub-continent. His attack on Hastings became less a search for truth than a personal and political vendetta, a propaganda campaign thinly coated with philosophical generalities. If Burke cannot be shown to have been guilty of deliberate distortion and falsification of the evidence then he can be shown to have indulged his passion against Hastings over and above the requirements of judicial deliberation. Burke was pleading a case and a cause before a public audience; although he stated that 'my motives are clear from private interest, and public malice',[5] his attitude towards the evidence was little short of cavalier: 'I know that the country (India) under his care is sacked and pillaged and I know he is the Government and I know a great deal more.'[6] But this conviction did not rest upon an empirical basis, 'We ought to be very careful not to charge what we are unable to prove.'[7] Burke declared that he was out to prove merely *a general evil intention*.[8] In stating the case for the impeachment before the House of Commons Burke was fully aware of tactical considerations:

> in order to bring about the great primary object of a strong case, I wish that the substance of the Charge should be either left to my own discretion, or, what I should like much better, that we should find some way of previously settling our plan of Conduct.[9]

---

[4] Burke to French Laurence, 10, 12 February 1797, *Correspondence*, IX, 238.
[5] Burke to Lord Thurlow, 4 December 1784, ibid., V, 198.
[6] Burke to Lord Thurlow, 14 December 1784, ibid., 204.
[7] Burke to Sir Philip Francis, 10 December 1785, loc. cit.
[8] Ibid.
[9] Burke to Henry Dundas, 25 March 1787, ibid., 312.

Furthermore, Burke was certainly aware of the value of ministerial help. He was prepared to abstain from much of his systematic opposition to Pitt's ministry for the sake of obtaining the help of the government.

> I shall therefore beg leave to add, that if ever there was a common National Cause totally seperated from Party it is this. A body of men, unlimited in a close connexion of common guilt and common apprehension of danger in the moment, with a strong and just confidence of future power if they escape it, and possessed of a measure of wealth and influence which perhaps you yourself have not calculated at any thing like its just magnitude, is not forming, but actually formed in this Country. This faction is at present ranged under Hastings as an Indian leader; and it will have very soon, if it has not already, an English Leader of considerable enterprise and no contemptible influence. If this faction should now obtain a Triumph it will be very quickly too strong for your Ministry. I will go further, and assert without the least shadow of hesitation, that they will turn out too strong for any one description of national interest that exists, or, on any probable speculation that can exist in our time. Nothing can rescue the Country out of their hands, but our vigorous use of the present fortunate moment, which if once lost is never to be recovered, of effectually breaking up this corrupt combination by effectually crushing the Leader and principal Members of the Corps.[10]

He naturally wanted to have his evidence presented to the Commons in the most favourable light. On one occasion he remarked to Dundas that 'Those Witnesses, upon whom we can personally prevail, must immediately come to Town to have their Evidence methodized.'[11]

In general, then, on matters pertaining to the impeachment Burke was prepared to seize every tactical advantage he could, losing no opportunity of blackening Hastings' character and expounding the enormity of his crimes. Much of Burke's Indian 'thought' then was expressed for motives of propaganda; it did not arise from philosophical considerations at all. Nevertheless, it is less the truth or falsehood of Burke's facts which needs to concern the present discussion than the ethical objectives towards which his Indian work was directed.

When this has been said, there is much in Burke's Indian thought

---

[10] Burke to Henry Dundas, 25 March 1787, *Correspondence*, 314.
[11] Ibid., 1 November 1787, ibid., 356.

that redounds to his credit. If he did not attain the highest standards of political honesty during the impeachment of Hastings then it remains true that Burke's motives were never self-interested. If he hated Warren Hastings, he hated not the man but the corruption Burke thought him to represent. A propagandist by his own admission, at least he sought to do his public duty, to awaken his fellow countrymen to the plight of the Indians. Burke was no crank, no alarmist. He was giving expression to fears and anxieties which had become increasingly common since the 1760s, especially the anxiety that the riches to be derived from the plunder of India might be directed towards the corruption of the British constitution. Although he exaggerated, he exaggerated in the best of causes, the cause of humanity and his exaggerations always had *some* basis in fact. He spent many long and weary hours preparing committee reports for the Commons on Indian affairs. (Burke was consequently one of the leading experts on Indian affairs of his political generation.)

What distinguished Burke from so many of his contemporaries was less his expert knowledge, however, than his consuming interest in Indian affairs. What accounts for the intensity of Burke's feelings for India? To some extent he was fascinated by the ancient order of Indian civilization and alarmed at what he took to be its desecration at the hands of the East India Company. He idealized Indian society and admired its law, its hierarchy and its religion. He argued that in spite of its turbulent history of invasion and war, India remained a Hindu polity in which the government behaved in accordance with the spirit and institutions of the people. Hastings threatened to destroy this Hindu polity and to innovate by introducing into India alien customs. Burke hated the idea of trying to anglicize India. It was the duty of the British to extend their oriental horizons, tolerate alien practices and promote their growth. Most important of all, the system of Indian law must not be destroyed. In India religious and civil laws were not separate systems, as in England, but part of one uniform system. It was to destroy the trust which parliament had vested in them for the company's servants to destroy that sensitive and delicate system. It was with this above all that Burke was fascinated, this above all he wished to preserve sound and entire.

Burke's early attitude towards India was determined largely by party considerations. In 1767 and 1773 he *defended* the East India Company from *ministerial* supervision. This was not the same as rejecting the notion of *parliamentary* supervision; for the moment, it appeared to Burke to be necessary to defend the independence of the company and to prevent its revenues falling into the hands of the crown. He attacked the Regulating Act[12] as 'contrary to the eternal laws of right and wrong – laws that ought to bind men, and above all men legislative assemblies'.[13] (We may be forgiven for not taking too seriously either on this occasion or later, during the impeachment, Burke's invocations of the Natural Law, preferring to recognize them as the rhetorical devices which Burke used to support his arguments whenever they needed reinforcement.)

Between 1773 and 1783 Burke completely shifted his ground on India. Growing familiarity with the subject brought him to fear the corrupting effects of Indian money upon the British constitution.[14] When the time came for parliament to renew the Regulating Act of 1773 (which had passed only for a duration of seven years) parliamentary discussion of the company's rule was inevitable. When the ministry of Lord North came out in support of the East India Company – and of Warren Hastings – the Rockinghamite opposition smelled a rat. Spurred on by the tales of Sir Philip Francis[15] who had his own personal axe to grind against Hastings, they dominated the deliberations of the Select Committee of 1780–1. At the same time as the Select Committee was sitting, a Secret Committee was also investigating Hastings' Governor Generalship of Bengal. By 1783 Burke had completely reversed his former role as defender of the East India Company. Burke was the driving force in the Select Committee which proceeded to publish no fewer than eleven reports. These were enough to remove any lingering doubts in his mind of Hastings' guilt. By 1783, therefore, Burke was prepared completely to reverse his earlier opinions. His India bills of 1783 proposed to do what he had criticized the North ministry for doing in 1773, namely, restraining the activities of the Company by bringing them under parliamentary surveillance. Burke had recourse to the argument that since 1773 the Company had broken the trust which parliament had entrusted to it and that therefore its charter ought to be revoked. We should be clear that Burke was perfectly prepared to rest the case for ministerial intervention upon a

---

[12] Lord North's Regulating Act of 1773 allowed the East India Company to continue to govern India for trading purposes, provided for a substantial loan to keep the Company solvent, reorganized the government of India and made it answerable to the British parliament.

[13] For Burke's early position on India see P. J. Marshall, *The Impeachment of Warren Hastings* (Oxford, 1965), 1–9.

[14] Burke to Rockingham, 27 April 1782, *Correspondence*, IV, 448–50.

[15] Francis became a committed member of Burke's party through his own personal vendetta against Hastings. His influence upon Burke, however, has been shown by Dr Marshall to have been exaggerated in the past, *The Impeachment of Warren Hastings*, 2–21, *passim*.

detailed scrutiny of the Company's record, not upon any abstract right. Burke thus proposed to bring the government of India under the control of a commission appointed by the ministry, not by the crown. His great speech on 1 December 1783 defended the measures and the philosophy behind them. Burke looked to his bills to cure the ills in the government of India. Of the two bills, the first vested the administration of the East India Company in seven commissioners and nine assistant commissioners, removable only by parliament. The second bill laid down regulations for the Company's servants to observe. The charge that the Indian policy of the coalition ministry was directed wholly towards maintaining Fox and his friends in office, suggested by a cursory glance at the first bill is, in fact, refuted by the details of the second.[16] Nevertheless, there is no escaping the fact that the coalition ministry was attacking chartered rights ostensibly in the party interest. The notorious overthrow of the ministry in the House of Lords[17] left Burke in no doubt that Hastings and the Company had directly interfered in British politics on this occasion. This conjecture became a certainty in Burke's mind after the defeat of his party at the 1784 election. He refused to accept the decision of the people as final and in 1786 he persuaded both the ministry of Pitt and the House of Commons to impeach Hastings, a significant achievement and a remarkable success for one man. Burke's lonely Indian crusade had begun.

The major theme of the impeachment was Burke's affirmation of the right of parliament not only to inquire into the affairs of the East India Company but also to exercise surveillance over the government of India. As we have seen, immediate political considerations together with a passionate humanitarianism inspired Burke's concern. There was one further motive: his belief that the British control of India might be endangered if the Company's arbitrary rule were allowed to continue. He said in December 1783 'that if we are not able to contrive some method of governing India *well*, which will not of necessity become the means of governing Great Britain *ill*, a ground is laid for their eternal separation'.[18] Misgovernment of India might, therefore, provoke a movement for Indian independence. All of this amounted to an overwhelming case for parliamentary surveillance. There was one critical difficulty with Burke's position. How could a good Rockingham Whig possibly profess any opinion which contravened the

---

[16] See the authoritative account in J. Cannon, *The Fox-North Coalition* (Cambridge, 1969), 106–23.

[17] Ibid., 124–44.

[18] *Works*, IV, 7 (Speech on the India Bill, 1 December 1783).

traditional Whig principle of the sanctity of chartered rights. Burke surmounted this difficulty by distinguishing between the *fundamental laws of the land* (such as Magna Carta) which were unalterable, and documents (like the charter of the East India Company) which were not. The former was a charter 'to restrain power and to destroy monopoly', the latter was a charter 'to establish monopoly and to create power'.[19] Burke did not question the rights of the Company as far as they went:

> Those who carry the rights and claims of the company the furthest, do not contend for more than this; and all this I freely grant. But granting all this, they must grant me in my turn, that all political power which is set over men, and that all privilege claimed or exercised in exclusion of them, being wholly artificial, and for so much a derogation from the natural quality of mankind at large, ought to be some way or other exercised ultimately for their benefit.[20]

In short, these rights were a trust. They were neither unlimited nor unrestricted. Burke laid it down that 'it is of the very essence of every trust to be rendered *accountable*; and even totally to *cease* when it substantially varies from the purposes for which alone it could have a lawful existence'.[21] And he went on to assert 'that if the abuse is proved, the contract is broken; and we re-enter into all our rights: that is, into the exercise of all our duties'. That is, Burke was out to promulgate, as he put it, 'the *magna charta* of Hindostan'.[22]

Burke thought it to be unsatisfactory to proceed upon a theoretical and arbitrary presumption about the rights and wrongs of the Company's rule. 'I feel an insuperable reluctance in giving my hand to destroy any established institution of government, upon a theory, however plausible it may be.'[23] Therefore to justify his taking the administration of India out of the hands of the Company Burke needed to prove that the evils perpetrated by the Company were of such a magnitude as to warrant any infringement of the charter.

> The abuse affecting this great object ought to be a great abuse. It ought to be habitual, and not accidental. It ought to be utterly incurable in the body as it now stands constituted. All this ought to be made as visible to me as the light of the sun, before I should strike off an atom of their charter.[24]

The first was self-evident in view of the extent of the Indian dominions

[19] *Works*, IV, 9.   [20] Ibid., 11.   [21] Ibid., 12.
[22] Ibid., 13.   [23] Ibid., 14.   [24] Ibid., I, 15.

and the size of the population. Burke sought to demonstrate the second proposition by proving firstly:

> that there is not a single prince, state, or potentate, great or small in India, with whom they have come into contact, whom they have not sold. I say sold, though sometimes they have not been able to deliver according to their bargain – Secondly I say, that there is not a single treaty, they have ever made, which they have not broken – Thirdly, I say, that there is not a single prince or state, who ever put any trust in the company, who is not utterly ruined; and that none are in any degree secure or flourishing, but in the exact proportion to their settled distrust an irreconcilable enmity to this nation.[25]

Burke demonstrated the validity of his propositions with a mass of evidence, most of it carefully chosen to fit his case, as indeed, such evidence had to be. He developed this theme further by showing that political disaster had been compounded by the commercial havoc which had been wreaked upon the natives of Bengal by the Company. Burke concluded in high dudgeon:

> In effect, Sir, every legal, regular authority in matters of revenue, of political administration, of criminal law, of civil law, in many of the most essential parts of military discipline, is laid level with the ground, and an oppressive, irregular, capricious, unsteady, rapacious, and peculating despotism without a direct disavowal of obedience to any authority at home, and without any fixed maxim, principle, or rule of proceeding, to guide them in India, is at present the state of your charter-government over great kingdoms.[26]

Long before the Coalition Ministry of 1783, therefore, Burke had made up his mind about the Company. In 1781, for example, he had declared that 'we find the Country infinitely injured, & the Treasures & revenues both of the Company & the subordinate powers wasted & decayed'.[27] Burke however, did not allow his party activities to prevent him from attending to the 'real wants of the people' of India.[28] In any case, as we have noticed on several occasions, his party favour was declining in the 1780s as his interest in India quickened. This did not prevent him from opposing Pitt's India Bill of 1784[29] on the

[25] *Works*, I, 21.   [26] Ibid., 93.
[27] Burke to Sir Thomas Rumbold, 23 March 1781, *Correspondence*, IV, 343–7.
[28] *Works*, IV, 122 (Speech on the India Bill, 1 December 1783).
[29] Pitt's India bill was similar to Burke's in many ways but left patronage in the hands of the Company subject only to a royal veto on appointments.

grounds that it 'put the whole East India Company into the hands of the Crown'.[30] Like many of his party colleagues, Burke came to believe a new myth after 1784 which in many ways was similar to the old Bute myth. Burke and others believed that after 1784 Pitt's government was using the influence of the crown to build up a new aristocracy in Britain, a new aristocracy which would replace the traditional elite of Britain, a new aristocracy based upon corruption and service in India. Burke confessed that the new court plan was more successful than ever the old one had been. The first victims of its corrupt and tyrannical success were the Indians. The only possible remedy was to reassert the function of parliament in exercising vigilance over the constituent parts of the constitution.

> It is difficult for the most wise and upright government to correct the abuses of remote, delegated power, productive of unmeasured wealth, and protected by the boldness and strength of the same ill-got riches. These abuses, full of their own wild native vigour, will grow and flourish under mere neglect. But where the supreme authority, not content with winking at the rapacity of its inferior instruments, is so shameless and corrupt as openly to give bounties and premiums for disobedience to its laws, when it will not trust to the activity of avarice in the pursuit of its own gains, when it secures public robbery by all the careful jealousy and attention with which it ought to protect property from such violence, the commonwealth then becomes totally perverted from its purposes; neither God nor man will long endure it, nor will it long endure itself. In that case, there is an unnatural infection, a pestilential taint fermenting in the constitution of society, which fever and convulsions of some kind or other must throw off.[31]

Burke's condemnation of Indian administration was, therefore, many-sided. The rule of the Company, in general, and of Hastings, in particular, was the very antithesis of what government ought to be because it did not consult the happiness of the governed. They did not govern the Indians with a due concern for their own experience and character. As he said of British politicians, 'We had not steadily before our eyes a general, comprehensive, well connected, and well-proportioned view of the whole of our dominions, and a just sense of their true bearings and relations.'[32] In 1781 he urged the Ministry of North to establish justice as the principle of all its proceedings as

[30] Speech on Pitt's India Bill, 16 January 1784, *Speeches*, II, 493.
[31] *Works*, IV, 318 (Speech on the Nabob of Arcot's Debts, 28 February 1785).
[32] Ibid.

the best method of ensuring the abiding loyalty of the Indians. As it was, government persecuted instead of protected the Indians. Parliament, the only recourse open to the Indians, was under the control of their oppressors after 1784. These oppressors were not the political agents of Great Britain at all.

It is not the English nation in India, it is nothing but a seminary for the occupation of offices. It is a nation of placemen, it is a republic, a body of people, a state, made up of magistrates, there is no one to watch the powers of office . . . being a kingdom of merchants, they are actuated by the spirit of the body – in other words, they consider themselves as having a common interest separate from that of the country in which they are, where there is no control of the persons that understand the language, and manners, and customs of the country.[33]

Hastings, of course, was the epitome of this avaricious separatism, this negation of government and of empire.

No account of his imperial philosophy can ignore the importance of the intense moral concern displayed by Burke on Indian affairs. His moral starting point was the proposition taken by Burke wittingly and directly from Montesquieu, unwittingly and indirectly from Grotius, that conquest does not permit arbitrary rule but rather carries with it moral duties and moral obligations 'to preserve the people in all their rights, laws and liberties' and 'to preserve and protect the people the same as if the Mogul's empire had existed, to observe the laws, rights, usages and customs of the natives, and to pursue their benefit in all things'.[34] Burke totally rejected Hastings' argument that the actions of Englishmen committed in India had to be judged according to local standards because 'the laws of morality are the same everywhere'.[35] Morality, for Burke, was not a question of geographical location. Furthermore, he brushed aside Hastings' further argument: that he had to govern as he found things. Burke saw no need for Hastings to capitalize on all manner of prevalent corruption.[36] The fact of conquest imposed considerable moral obligations upon the conqueror. Although conquest gave him considerable arbitrary discretion in matters of government, the greater the discretion, the greater the compulsion to deal justly. Burke denied that it had ever been part of the legitimate policy of the Company to wield arbitrary power. Not only *had* it never been, it *never could be*. The Company had never had

[33] Speech on Opening the Articles of Impeachment, 15 February 1788, *Speeches*, IV, 312–13.
[34] Ibid., 308–9.   [35] Ibid., 305.   [36] Ibid., 375 (18 February 1788).

such powers to wield. It had never had them because parliament had never given them and never could.

My Lords, the East India Company have not arbitrary power to give him; the king has no arbitrary power to give him; your Lordships have not; nor the Commons, nor the whole legislature. We have no arbitrary power to give, because arbitrary power is a thing which neither any man can hold nor any man can give. No man can lawfully govern himself according to his own will; much less can one person be governed by the will of another. We are all born in subjection, – all born equally, high and low, governors and governed, in subjection to one great, immutable, pre-existent law, prior to all our devices and prior to all our contrivances, paramount to all our ideas and all our sensations, antecedent to our very existence, by which we are knit and connected in the eternal frame of the universe, out of which we cannot stir. This great law does not arise from our conventions or compacts; on the contrary, it gives to our conventions and compacts all the force and sanction they can have. It does not arise from our vain institutions. Every good gift of God; all power is of God; and He who has given the power, and from whom alone it originates, will never suffer the exercise of it to be practised upon any less solid foundation than the power itself. If, then, all dominion of man over man is the effect of the Divine disposition, it is bound by the eternal laws of Him that gave it.[37]

Nobody can deny the sincerity and the moral force of passages such as this. To acknowledge these characteristics does not, however, itself clarify the status of the moral argument that Burke used and, in particular, it does not reveal the significance which attaches to his appeals to the Natural Law.

It is worth repeating what we said earlier: that Burke's appeals to the Natural Law ought not to be 'lifted' from their place in a speech or even in the impeachment as a whole. Their rhetorical impact is completely lost if they are treated as 'quotations' or as academic data which, taken together 'prove' Burke's attachment to the Natural Law. It is worth repeating that Burke never believed that he could convince the court of the illegality of Hastings' actions. His intention was to persuade the world that those same actions, while not illegal, were both immoral and illegitimate. To effect such a persuasion was the function of Burke's invocations of the Natural Law during the trial. The Natural Law was needed – increasingly – as the trial wore on, as

[37] Speech on Opening the Articles of Impeachment, 15 February 1788, *Speeches*, IV, 308–9.

a rhetorical device because the managers found that more and more of their evidence was ruled to be inadmissible by the judges according to precedent. It was convenient – perhaps necessary – for Burke to establish another standard by which his evidence would not be dismissed. Sincere, Burke undoubtedly was in his condemnation of Hastings but that there was an element of calculation in his rhetoric will be denied only by his most unthinking admirers.[38] The theatrical impact of his Natural Law perorations was just as important as their logical precision. Indeed, it was probably far more important. It was all very well for Burke to tell the judges that Hastings' crimes were 'not against morals, but against those eternal laws of justice which you are assembled here to assert'.[39] But what were 'those eternal laws of justice'? The judges did not know and they cannot have been much enlightened by Burke's explanation:

> There is one thing, and one thing only, which defies all mutation that which existed before the world, and will survive the fabric of the world itself; I mean justice; that justice, which, emanating from the Divinity, has a place in the breast of every one of us, gives us for our guide with regard to ourselves and with regard to others, and which will stand after this globe is burned to ashes, our advocate or our accuser before the great Judge, when He comes to call upon us for the tenor of a well-spent life.[40]

Until – and unless – such passages are endowed with some meaning, Burke's appeals to the Natural Law must be treated with considerable reserve.

In fact, none of the great 'moral' themes of the impeachment of Warren Hastings rested upon a Natural Law basis. The idea that the government of the empire ought to be conducted in the interests of the governed, that government should act within the law, that conquest carried with it responsibilities, that government ought to be carried on in accordance with the spirit and traditions of the governed – these commonplaces of the British (and European) constitutional tradition were taken over by Burke and applied to the problems of India.

Too much can be – and has been – claimed for Burke's Indian crusade. Morley, for example, asserted that Burke won a new status for Indians in the empire and overthrew a corrupt system of government. Burke did nothing of the kind. The abuses in the government of India against which Burke raised his voice were already well known

---

[38] Speech on Opening the Articles of Impeachment, 18 February 1788, *Speeches*, IV, 374.

[39] Ibid., 303–4 (15 February 1788).

[40] *Works*, XVI, 417 (Speech at the Close of the Impeachment, 16 June 1794).

to the public; even while the impeachment was dragging on, steps were being taken to ameliorate them. Pitt's India Bill of 1784 permanently established parliamentary control of the East India Company and the beginning of Cornwallis' regime in the following year marked the inauguration of a new phase in the life of 'John Company'. We should be prepared to place Burke's Indian crusade in its proper perspective in both British and Indian history. We should be prepared to acknowledge, and thus to try to understand, the personal and political motives which prompted Burke's inexhaustible industry. We should, moreover, attempt to relate his Indian thought to other aspects of his imperial philosophy. And if that philosophy reflected the variations in the nature of the imperial problem in different parts of the empire then no more can be expected from the 'philosopher in action'.

Chapter VI

The French Revolution

In Burke's French revolutionary thought political philosophy became incidental to a generalized view of man and society. Although his French thought was, to a large extent, consistent with his earlier constitutional and imperial theories, it is much too facile a view to contend that Burke's later thought 'arose out of' his earlier ideas or that it was in some way 'an extension of' them. For Burke now had a new objective: to defend the *ancien régime* in France and in Europe. To achieve this objective it was necessary for him to demonstrate that radical political change was not only unworkable but, in the context of the *ancien régime*, positively undesirable. He therefore underlined the danger of innovation and disruption which might be thrust upon a social system by introducing new and alien elements into an old social and political fabric. In one sense, Burke's historical perspective was limited. Although he was aware of the great developments of history and the variations of culture and society between one continent and another he could neither see that the England of Pitt and Rockingham was dying nor that a new commercial and industrial society was already emerging. The central feature of Burke's French revolutionary thought was his concern to preserve the old society.

In this role, his thinking was just as abstract and as speculative as that of the writers whom he attacked. He hated the radical authors because their works weakened the old prejudices and habits which formed the psychological foundations of the *ancien régime*. Burke's assumptions that the life of the individual is rooted in the life of the state and that the life of the state is rooted in its history were just as arbitrary as comparable assumptions made by the 'Jacobin' theorists whom he so vehemently denounced. Abstract and speculative his philosophy might be, Burke deliberately, however, chose to sustain the role of critic of contemporary thought. His revolutionary thought was his reaction to the current enlightenment philosophy of religion, of society and of man. The Enlightenment elicited deep intellectual anxieties in Burke's mind to which he gave expression in an anti-revolutionary philosophy. This proceeded from an anti-rationalist position. Liberty, for example, was not an abstract proposition but a social reality. Property was not to be regarded as a mental construct. It was, in practical terms, the bulwark of the social order. Inevitably, then, Burke's anti-rationalism strengthened his enduring presumption in favour of any established government or existing institution. The state thus became a vehicle for maintaining and for transmitting the structure and traditions of a society irrespective of popular sentiment. He proclaimed that in his French writings 'He proposed to convey to a foreign people, not his own ideas, but the prevalent opinions and sentiments of a nation, renowned for wisdom, and celebrated in all ages for a well understood and well regulated love of freedom.'[1] But he was speaking only for the propertied class of his country. He did not speak to and he did not write for the man who read Paine's *Rights of Man*. Indeed, it was man's duties rather than his rights which impressed him during the 1790s. In a very real sense, then, Burke was the spokesman of the *ancien régime* in Europe during the revolutionary crisis.

The French Revolution occurred when Burke's career – and his morale – were at their very nadir, and when the impeachment of Warren Hastings, upon which he had pinned all his hopes, was dragging along tediously. Even worse, the king's illness of the winter of 1788–9 had found Burke's party divided and utterly incapable of taking political advantage of the situation. It was less his party's failure which distressed Burke – he had grown accustomed to failure during the past twenty years – than the failure of his party colleagues to uphold the traditional Whig doctrine of hereditary succession during the Regency crisis of 1788–9.[2]

As to the Prince, I found him deeply concerned that the Ideas of an elective Crown should not prevail. He had experienced, and you had all of you fully experienced the Peril of these doctrines on the question of the Regency. . . . I supported the Princes Title to the

---

[1] *Works*, VI, 76 (Appeal from the New to the Old Whigs, 1791).

[2] The king's illness during the winter of 1788–9 threatened to create a vacancy upon the throne. The natural candidate for the Regency, the Prince of Wales, was closely associated with the opposition and there is little doubt that a Regency would have resulted in Pitt's resignation and the formation of a ministry under the Duke of Portland, Rockingham's successor, and led, in the Commons, by Fox. There is a good account of the crisis in J. W. Derry, *The Regency Crisis, and the Whigs, 1788–9* (Cambridge, 1963).

Regency upon the Principle of his Hereditary Right to the Crown: and I endeavoured to explode the false Notions, drawn from what has been stated as the Revolution Maxims. . . . I endeavoured to shew, that the Hereditary succession could not be supported, whilst a person who had the Interest in it, was, during a virtual interregnum, excluded from the Government; and that the direct tendency of the measure, as well as the grounds upon which it was argued, went to make the Crown itself elective contrary (as I contended) to the fundamental Settlement made after the Revolution.[3]

Burke bitterly resented his party's inability to support the basic principles upon which it had been founded. He had become irascible, tetchy and resentful, an object of ridicule and a figure of fun in the House of Commons. Apparently he had outlived his political usefulness. An embarrassment to his colleagues, isolated and with no political future, Burke had sunk to the lowest point in his career. The revolution transformed that reputation and saved it from the relative obscurity to which Burke appeared to be destined.

More than any other aspect of his thought, Burke's French ideas need to be related to the political circumstances of the time if they are to be understood. For all its generalizations and its defence of the *ancien régime* in France, the *Reflections on the Revolution in France* (1790) were indisputably directed towards a *British* rather than a French or European audience and to a particular domestic situation. Burke was worried about the growth of radicalism in his own party and in writing the *Reflections* he was attempting to alert the party leaders, and, indirectly, the Prince of Wales, to the dangers to which radical opinions, however innocent and however sincerely held, could run. Indeed, Burke was mainly concerned with the French Revolution as a practical example and a timely illustration of the dangers of radicalism to Englishmen. He was, at first, more concerned with the practical *effects* of revolution than with its causes or its ideological motivations. His earliest, serious reservation about the revolution was his fear that the National Assembly would not be strong enough to function as a government. This was the rock upon which the ship of the *ancien régime* had foundered: 'I very much question, whether they are in a condition to exercise any function of decided authority'.[4] The Assembly would be too weak to assert itself against mob rule. Burke's earliest doubts about the revolution, therefore, sprang from his belief

[3] Edmund Burke to William Weddell, 31 January 1792, *Correspondence*, VII, 58.
[4] Burke to William Weddell, 27 September 1789, ibid., VI, 25.

that democracy in France would not give rise to stability. This caution ripened into a conviction that the organs of the revolutionary state would become subjected by degrees to the pressures of mob rule and military dictatorship. Hence Burke condemned the French Revolution because it had destroyed liberty ('the birthright of our species'[5]), because it had failed to maintain the conditions in which a free man could exist 'in a perfect state of legal security, with regard to his life, to his property, to the uncontrolled disposal of his Person, to the free use of his Industry and his faculties.'[6] Yet he made neither a constructive suggestion nor proposal to assist the French to overcome their fortuitous inability as a nation to establish liberty. The reason for their failure was not hard to find: Burke believed that the revolution *must* fail because it derived its inspiration from a false and abstract philosophy. 'It is with man in the concrete, it is with common human life and human Actions you are to be concerned. . . . Never wholly separate in your Mind the merits of any Political Question from the Men who are concerned in it.'[7]

Up to this point, his intention was to dissuade his fellow-countrymen from imitating the French. Then, in January 1790, Burke stumbled across what he could regard as nothing but definite proof that a plot existed. For none other than Thomas Paine chose to confide in Burke his thorough approval of the revolution and his sincere wish that 'The Revolution in France is certainly a Forerunner to other Revolutions in Europe.' He expressed the wish that future alliances in Europe should be alliances of the peoples of Europe against the courts of Europe.[8] This removed any lingering doubts that Burke might still have entertained about the revolution.

> In all appearance, the new system is a most bungling, and unwork-
> manlike performance, I confess I see no principle of coherence,
> co-operation, or just subordination of parts in this whole project,
> nor any the least aptitude to the condition and wants of the state
> to which it is applied, nor any thing well imagined for the formation,
> provision, or direction of a common force. The direct contrary
> appears to me.[9]

What most concerned Burke, however, was the possibility that there existed in Britain a faction dedicated to emulating the French. A few

[5] Burke to Charles-Jean Francois Depont, November 1789, *Correspondence* VI, 39–50.
[6] Ibid.   [7] Ibid.
[8] Thomas Paine to Burke, 17 January 1790, ibid., 67–75.
[9] Burke to an unidentified recipient, January 1790, ibid., 78–81.

weeks later, on 9 February, Burke announced to a surprised House of Commons – and an even more astonished opposition party – his hostility to the French faction in England who wished to level the state. He concluded by warning the Whig party that if it professed support for democratic principles then he would break with it. Edmund Burke's counter-revolution had begun.[10]

Towards the end of the same year he published his *Reflections*. His purpose in giving the tract to the world was to confirm his fellow-countrymen in their belief in the aristocratic, hereditary nature of the British constitution and to demonstrate its incompatibility with the revolutionary principles of France. In August 1791 he issued his *Appeal from the New to the Old Whigs* in which he exposed the principles of the radical wing in the opposition party, demonstrating their inconsistency with those of the old 'Revolution' Whigs. Burke warned one of his readers against taking the 'Appeal' too philosophically, however: 'But surely you forget, that I was throwing out reflexions upon a political event, and not reading a lecture upon theories and principles of Government.'[11] The outbreak of war between France, on the one hand, and Austria and Prussia, on the other, in the spring of 1792 confirmed the prediction which he had already made: that the revolution could only be saved by a foreign war. Yet the war introduced a novel and dangerous factor into the situation. It raised the political temperature and quickened the speed of developments inside France. The imprisonment of the French king in August 1792 touched a chord of hysteria in Burke. By then, he had noted ominously, the French had begun to regard the war as a messianic crusade to spread revolution throughout Europe and to destroy its christian, feudal foundations. Burke viewed the war as an attack upon the ideal of a mixed, aristocratic government. Without the aristocratic principle, Burke believed, 'every Dominion must become a mere despotism of the Prince, or the brutal Tyranny of a ferocious and atheistic populace'.[12] He was horrified at the imprisonment of Louis XVI in August 1792.

This last Revolution, whatever name it may assume, at present bears no one Character of a National Act. It is the Act only of some desperate Persons, Inhabitants of one City only, instigating and hiring at an enormous Expence, the lowest of the people, to destroy the Monarch and Monarchy, with whatever else is respectable in Society. Not one Officer of the National Guards of Paris, which

[10] 9 February 1790, *The Parliamentary History*, XXVIII, 337–73.
[11] Burke to W. C. Smith, 22 July 1791, *Correspondence*, VI, 303–4.
[12] Burke to Richard Burke Junior, 29 July 1792, ibid., VII, 160.

Officers are composed of nothing higher than good Tradesmen, has appeared in this business. It is not yet adopted throughout France by any one Class of People. No regular Government of any Country has yet an Object with which they can decently treat in France, or to which they can rationally make any official Declaration whatsoever.[13]

Burke openly proclaimed the doctrine that Britain ought to intervene militarily in France. If she did so, she would be merely following precedents which had saved the constitution in the past.

But an abstract principle of public law, forbidding such interference, is not supported by the reason of that law, nor by the Authorities on the Subject nor by the practice of this Kingdom, nor by that of any civilized Nation in the World. This Nation owes its Laws and Liberties, his Majesty owes the Throne on which he sits, to the contrary principle. The several Treaties of Guarantee to the protestant Succession, more than once reclaimed, affirm the principle of interference which in a manner forms the basis of the public Law of Europe.[14]

Britain's failure to intervene would only fill the Jacobins with fresh hope and renewed enthusiasm.

Burke rested his case and waited for events to justify his warnings. The September Massacres, the trial and execution of the French king and French threats against England led gruadually but inevitably to the outbreak of war between the two countries early in 1793. Burke was keen to impress upon the government of William Pitt that the war ought neither to be a war for trade nor merely a war of national independence but a crusade against the principle of Jacobinism itself. The government would pursue a short-sighted policy of national aggrandizement at its peril. The world must be made safe for the *ancien régime*. It would not be safe until Jacobinism had been uprooted in France itself. Thus in 1795, when war weariness led the British to negotiate with the French, Burke was nearly beside himself at the prospect of negotiating peace with a regicide republic. Peace with France could not be permanent because it was the intention of the Jacobins to destroy Britain. Peace was in the interests of the Jacobins only in so far as it would give them time to regroup and rest before renewing their assault upon property and hierarchy throughout Europe. Until his death in 1797, Burke never ceased to advocate

[13] Burke to Lord Grenville, 18 August 1792, *Correspondence*, VII, 174.
[14] Ibid., 176.

bloody war upon the armies of Jacobinism. His counter-revolution had in effect become a crusade.

The motivation for and the context of Burke's French thought were overtly propagandist. Burke's French revolutionary thought, it should be remembered, was intended to be a refutation of the radical theories of radicals, such as the unfortunate Dr Richard Price, of whom Burke made such an example in *The Reflections*. Burke reacted instinctively against what he took to be their superficial commitment to the idea of the inexorable progress of society and the inevitable perfectibility of man. The historical method which he adopted in many of his writings was curiously circular. It is difficult to disentangle his historical method from his political theory. Burke found the vindication of his appeals to history in history itself and the historical conclusions which he reached affected his method. For he derived from his study of history the conclusion that rational speculation about the destiny of states was a fruitless and unprofitable undertaking; schemes by abstract thinkers to plan a utopian society must come to naught because they rest on the assumption that the life of states can be ordered, predicted and arranged, that the beneficial effect of a reform, or group of reforms, can be guaranteed. As he had been saying for years, not only the institutions and the customs but also the 'spirit' of a people are the products of the ages. Burke thus tied the present closely to the past and drew a discreet veil over the future. His philosophy, because of its historical orientation, was profoundly conservative. Burke's reforming impulses were directed towards restoring the legacy of the past and freeing it of corruption. His stress upon history, tradition and prescription inclined him to fear the consequences of abstract philosophy: 'The triumph of philosophy is the universal conflagration of Europe',[15] thundered Burke.

The cardinal error of the Jacobins was to ignore history and to apply the principles of science to the unquantifiable matter of social life. They stressed the physical and material side of man's nature to the exclusion of those intangible aspects of the personality which render men human. Furthermore, Burke professed to distrust 'reason' because it was nothing more than the speculations of particular men and he saw no reason to endow their ponderings with an infallible status. Burke was familiar with the view that the reason affected only a small part of man's nature, that instinct and emotion impinged upon the rest and that the kingdom of reason touched only a small part of human action. 'Politics ought to be adjusted, not to human reasonings, but to human

[15] *Works*, VII, 324 (Preface to William Burke's Translation of Brissot's Address to his Constituents).

nature: of which the reason is but a part, and by no means the greatest part', he had stated as early as 1769.[16] This meant that apparently 'irrational' aspects of men's behaviour had their importance. For example, customs and traditions, for Burke, were not simply medieval relics to be retained for the sake of nostalgia or antiquarianism. They acquired their own raison d'etre through their existence time out of mind. The cumulative wisdom of successive generations had recognized their value and they had, consequently, survived.[17]

We must be extremely careful, however, of regarding Burke as an 'anti-rationalist' philosopher. Although he would, no doubt, have been glad to be regarded in this manner by posterity we should notice that his anti-rationalism does not stretch very far. Certain aspects of the political philosophy which Burke expounded in the 1790s arose from a 'rationalist' style of argument. To some extent, this tactic was forced upon him because he had to meet and refute the contract theories of radical writers, the starting point of their (not his) philosophy. Burke adopted the view that in the matter of the contract man has no choice, that the nature of the contract arises from the nature of man himself and thus it lasts for ever. Burke's contract theory freezes social relationships in their 'original' state.

> Once social relations had been settled upon some compact, tacit or expressed, there is no power existing of force to alter it, without the breach of the covenant, or the consent of all the parties. Such is the nature of a contract. And the votes of a majority of the people, whatever their infamous flatterers may teach in order to corrupt their minds, cannot alter the moral any more than they can alter the physical essence of things. The people are not to be taught to think lightly of their engagements to their governours; else they teach governours to think lightly of their engagements towards them. In that kind of game in the end the people are sure to be losers.[18]

For Burke these propositions were unchangeable; men have power to alter neither their duties nor the morality which dictates them. The obligations of the contract are thus timeless.

> Society is indeed a contract. Subordinate contracts for objects of mere occasional interest may be dissolved at pleasure – but the state ought not to be considered as nothing better than a partnership

[16] R. R. Fennessy, *Burke, Paine and the Rights of Man* (The Hague, 1963), 62.
[17] Ibid., 62–75 *passim.*, for a detailed critique of Burke's idea of rights.
[18] *Works*, VI, 201–2 (*Appeal*).

agreement in a trade of pepper and coffee, calico or tobacco, or some other such low concern, to be taken up for a little temporary interest, and to be dissolved by the fancy of the parties. It is to be looked on with other reverence; because it is not a partnership in things subservient only to the gross animal existence of a temporary and perishable nature. It is a partnership in all science; a partnership in all art; a partnership in every virtue, and in all perfection. As the ends of such a partnership cannot be obtained in many generations, it becomes a partnership not only between those who are living, but between those who are living, those who are dead, and those who are to be born. Each contract of each particular state is but a clause in the great primaeval contract of eternal society, linking the lower with the higher natures, connecting the visible and invisible world, according to a fixed compact sanctioned by the inviolable oath which holds all physical and all moral natures, each in their appointed place. This law is not subject to the will of those, who by an obligation above them, and infinitely superior, are bound to submit their will to that law.[19]

Burke's contract, then, is quite different to the logical construct of other writers. It is permanent, binding and unchangeable. It also has a moral sanction, since duties, arising from the contract 'arise from the relation of man to man, and the relation of man to God, which relations are not matters of choice'.[20]

The 'state of nature', for Burke, was therefore a state of inhuman anarchy to which man *must* not choose to return. He asserted that human institutions, far from imposing artificial restraints upon man, as many enlightenment writers declared, liberated him from the anarchy of the state of nature and enabled him in an orderly freedom to develop his faculties. Burke thus freed himself from what had been one of the traditional concerns of political philosophy: speculation concerning the origins of society derived from abstract notions of the state of nature. Burke was content to draw certain general principles from his discussion of the state of nature. His idea of contract and his idea of the state of nature led him to the conclusion that government and its obligations were not determined by its origins but by the nature of man and his moral duties. Indeed, he considered discussion of the origins of government futile. In a well known passage, Burke declared: 'The foundations, on which obedience to governments is

[19] *Works*, V, 183–4 (*Reflections on the Revolution in France, 1790*).
[20] Ibid., VI, 204–5 (*Appeal*).

founded, are not to be constantly discussed. That we are here, supposes the discussion already made and the dispute settled.'[21] Thus he would give a presumption in favour of established institutions to govern the individual 'until some intolerable grievance shall make us know that it does not answer its end, and will submit neither to reformation nor restraint'.[22]

These characteristic conceptions of contract and the state of nature were almost certainly intended by Burke to be a rebuttal of the fashionable ideas of the enlightenment. In departing, as it were, from the Age of Reason, Burke opened up the field of political science and began to penetrate its depths. His state of nature was not the pre-contractual situation of anarchic man but the post-contractual state of civil society. Burke shifted philosophy away from the logical and legal manner of thinking which had traditionally characterized its discussions. This he did because he regarded such questions as problems not of logic or of law but of practice, that is, of politics. Burke, therefore, rejected entirely the fashionable concept of nature. In the sense that Burke's 'nature' was somewhat more realistic and historical than many contemporary versions of nature then he may be regarded as less speculative than his radical opponents. At least, he succeeded in conforming nature to man and exploded the enlightenment's attempt to force a mythical man to conform to a non-existent nature. It is hardly surprising that his version of 'natural rights' did not even mention the typical 'pre-social' rights of rebellion and resistance to authority. On the contrary, men were bound to obey legitimate, i.e. prescriptive, authority. Burke's natural rights amounted to the normal benefits of social living, those of order, security, justice and peaceful possession of property and labour.[23] The purpose of the state was to preserve those rights. These were social rights. They did not include political power. Rights to political power were not 'natural'. Such rights were acquired not through the contract but through experience (i.e. history) and according to circumstances. Rights do not exist apart from society. They evolved through time with customary obligation, traditional morality and established institutions. Burke had no time for those theorists who were for ever stressing the rights of the individual at the expense of the power of the state. Natural rights could only exist in society; they are not anterior to it. For Edmund Burke, then, rights

---

[21] Speech on the Unitarians' Petition, 11 May 1792, *Works*, X, 51–2.
[22] Ibid., 52–3.
[23] This idea of natural rights owes much to Montesquieu. See F. T. M. Fletcher, *Montesquieu and English Politics, 1750–1800* (1939), 109–13.

were not legal or personal matters, but the residue of experience and time, enshrined in the institutional apparatus of society.

The totality of a society existed in time through prescription and inheritance. But since rights depended upon society, Burke believed that society had to be preserved if natural rights were to survive. Because European society was traditionally elitist, Burke, in defending that society, was, inevitably, defending the prescriptive ownership of property and the prescriptive title to political authority of a few hundred aristocratic families. For example, one of the most important of Burke's natural rights was the right to own property. In the context of Europe at the end of the eighteenth century, the right to property, and the right to transmit property by inheritance and by prescription, meant that those who already enjoyed the ownership of property would be the chief beneficiaries of Burke's crusade. The events of the 1790s, of course, reinforced Burke's elitism. The lynch-pin of this elitism was his belief that immemorial possession legitimized both the ownership of property and titles to political authority, no matter how that property or that authority had originally been acquired.[24] Prescription served for Burke the purpose which natural rights served for the radicals. It legitimized authority. This is the crucially important function of his conception of prescription in his philosophy:

It is not calling the landed estates, possessed by old *prescriptive rights*, the 'accumulations of ignorance and superstition', that can support me in shaking that grand title, which supersedes all other titles, and which all my studies of general jurisprudence have taught me to consider as one principal cause of the formation of states; I mean the ascertaining and securing *prescription*. But these are donations made in the 'ages of ignorance and superstition'. Be it so. It proves that these donations were made long ago; and this is *prescription*; and this gives right and title. It is possible that many estates about you were originally obtained by arms, that is, by violence, a thing almost as bad as superstition, and not much short of ignorance but it is *old violence*; and that which might be wrong in the beginning, is consecrated by time, and becomes lawful. This may be superstition in me, and ignorance; but I had rather remain in ignorance and superstition than be enlightened and purified out of the first principles of law and natural justice. I never will suffer you, if I can help it, to be deprived of the well-earned fruits of your industry, because others may want your fortune more than you do,

[24] P. Lucas, 'Edmund Burke's Doctrine of Prescription or an Appeal from the New to the Old Lawyers', *Historical Journal*, XI (1968), 35-9.

and may have laboured, and do now labour, in vain, to acquire even a subsistence. Nor on the contrary, if success had less smiled on your endeavours, and you had come home insolvent, would I take from any 'pampered and luxurious lord' in your neighbourhood one acre of his land, or one spoon from his sideboard, to compensate your losses, though incurred (as they would have been incurred) in the course of a well-spent, virtuous and industrious life. God is the distributor of his own blessings. I will not impiously attempt to usurp his throne, but will keep according to the subordinate place and trust in which he has stationed me, to secure the order of property which I find established in my country.[25]

Burke's view of the historical process, his conception of nature and his scepticism of 'reason' determine his idea of the state. His prescriptive conception of the state did not permit him to express anything like an 'idea of progress', or even an evolutionary or linear view of history. His idea of the state is 'organic' in the sense that he appealed to experience and recognized that states and institutions can and must change but it remains true that this change was not to be directed to a future ideal. Political change, for Burke then, operated correctly when it restored the state to its original nature. In short, Burke had no vision of a different political or social order. Not only that. His very instincts tended towards restoration and conservation: his philosophy was so solidly based upon prescription that his idea of the state acquired a tremendous inertia.

His idea of the state was also something of a curiosity in European thought. It is different to the customary 'state' inhabited by eighteenth-century philosophers. It is even different to the 'state' inhabited by Burke himself earlier in his life. In his later writings he stressed the powers of the state; in his earlier writings he had emphasized the rights of the individual against those of the state. Burke's 'state' of the 1790s was a very different thing from the 'state' of Locke, Montesquieu and most of the radicals (who contented themselves with a state in which the central government exercised very little authority; little more, in fact, than the regulation of diplomatic affairs and the currency). In the 1790s he strongly reaffirmed his belief that the state was a trust based upon heredity, property and law. As the role of the state in his political thought loomed larger, his conception grew of its delicacy and complexity. 'Government is a contrivance of human wisdom to provide for human wants', he wrote.[26] The organization of a state and

[25] Burke to Captain Thomas Mercer, 26 February 1790, *Correspondence*, VI, 95. [26] *Works*, V, 122 (*Reflections*).

its government was 'a matter of the most delicate and complicated skill'.[27] It followed, then, that one man, or one group of men, ought not lightly to pull down what the centuries had fashioned, in accordance with the wants and needs of a people.

Burke emphatically did not believe that government ought to be conducted according to the wishes of the majority. When the people demanded change such change must be pursued in accordance with the political and social context of the country concerned, its history, traditions and customs. Institutions must be reformed in accordance with their original principles, spirit and purposes. Reform should preserve rather than destroy. There was another reason why Burke closed his ears to the voice of the majority. Political wisdom was not a matter of collecting voices and counting heads. In 1791 he wrote: 'Political problems do not primarily concern truth or falsehood. They relate to good or evil.'[28] All of this did not mean that Burke was opposed to reform. For much of his career, indeed, he was far in advance of public opinion. What he would not allow was radical change based upon the will of the multitude whose effects could not be foreseen and which might introduce alien principles and damaging innovations in ancient polities. The art of the reformer was a fine and delicate art which required a leader of profound wisdom to decide what needed reform, when and how it should be accomplished, what priorities should be observed and how to apply the principles of equity and justice. Reform should proceed less from will than from necessity, less from theory than from experience. Burke, clearly, left little room for reform in his later political theory, although he by no means ruled it out altogether. At a time when established institutions throughout Europe were under assault he had, no doubt, little enthusiasm for encouraging further attacks upon them.

Consequently, Burke left little room in his doctrines for rebellion. He conceded that if the existence of society itself were threatened by its leaders and if means of effecting peaceful political change had been exhausted, then, and only then, rebellion was permissible. This was scarcely more than acknowledging that a society ought to be allowed to survive. In practice, and in the case of France, Burke appeared to rule out rebellion if a constitution existed which could be reformed and, ultimately, become the vehicle for political change. In his Letter to a Member of the National Assembly (January 1791) Burke stated that 'the attempt to oppress, degrade, impoverish, confiscate, and extinguish the original gentlemen, and landed property of a whole

[27] *Works*, VI, 210 (*Appeal*).
[28] Ibid., V, 125 (*Reflections*).

nation cannot be justified under any form it may assume'.[29] But presumably the abuses of the *ancien régime* could! It is difficult to escape the conclusion that, in his fear of revolution, Burke overlooked just those aspects of the society of the *ancien régime* which had made revolution or the danger of revolution possible. In particular, he was quite unwilling to concede the legitimacy of changes in the distribution of wealth and changes in the socio-economic structure of Europe.

Burke's French thought was an even more vigorous defence of elitism than his earlier thought had been. Yet he did all that he could to conceal the fact. He denied that he wished to 'confine power, authority, and distinction to blood and names, and titles. . . . There is no qualification for government but virtue and wisdom, actual or presumptive.'[30] Nevertheless, he insisted that the road to power ought not to be paved too smoothly. Although he made a few gestures in the direction of merit, Burke was quite content to preserve the system of privilege in Europe and to tolerate its class distinctions and its other inequalities. Indeed, he thought it a characteristic feature of property to be unevenly distributed. 'Its defensive power is weakened as it is diffused'[31] for the greater the diffusion of property the greater will be the envy it creates among men jealous of their neighbour's portion. Burke not only tolerated this inequality but thought its perpetuation through inheritance 'one of the most valuable and interesting circumstances belonging to it'.[32] We should be clear why Burke defended the rule of a small, propertied class. It was not because the rule of that class acted as a barrier against totalitarianism – the eighteenth-century state was too weak to establish a centralized, totalitarian structure – but because it acted as a barrier against mob rule and anarchy. He contemplated France with horror, where the multitude had succeeded in destroying the rule of a propertied minority, but the French people had not received one square metre of the estates of the aristocracy, church and monarchy.[33] The old society had been succeeded not by democracy or equality but by slavery, famine and war.

Burke's defence of a 'natural aristocracy', therefore, is integral to his conception of social stability, 'To be honoured and even privileged by the laws, opinions, and inveterate usages of our country, growing out of the prejudice of ages, has nothing to provoke horror and indignation in any man.'[34] Burke saw order and hierarchy, privilege and inequality, in all social systems and thus in all governments. The mass

[29] *Works*, VI, 4–5 (Letter to a Member of the National Assembly, 1791).
[30] Ibid., V, 106 (*Reflections*).   [31] Ibid., 108.   [32] Ibid., 108.
[33] Speech at the Opening of the Session, 13 December 1792, *Speeches*, IV, 76.
[34] *Works*, V, 254 (*Reflections*).

of the people should rest content in their position of natural sub-ordination. 'They must respect that property of which they cannot partake.'[35] Burke's famous defence of the 'natural aristocracy' is perhaps one of the most open admissions of elitism in the whole of British philosophy.

A true natural aristocracy is not a separate interest in the state, or separable from it. It is an essential integrant part of any large body rightly constituted. It is formed out of a class of legitimate presumptions, which, taken as generalities, must be admitted for actual truths. To be bred in a place of estimation; to see nothing low and sordid from one's infancy; to be taught to respect one's self; to be habituated to the censorial inspection of the publick eye, to look early to publick opinion; to stand upon such elevated ground as to be enabled to take a large view of the wide-spread and infinitely diversified combinations of men and affairs in a large society; to have leisure to read, to reflect, to converse; to be enabled to draw the court and attention of the wise and learned wherever they are to be found; – to be habituated in armies to command and to obey; to be taught to despise danger in the pursuit of honour and duty, to be formed to the greatest degree of vigilance, foresight, and circumspection, in a state of things in which no fault is committed with impunity, and the slightest mistakes draw on the most ruinous consequences – to be led to a guarded and regulated conduct, from a sense that you are considered as an instructor of your fellow-citizens in their highest concerns, and that you act as a reconciler between God and man – to be employed as an administrator of law and justice, and to be thereby amongst the first benefactors to mankind – to be a professor of high science, or of liberal and ingenuous art – to be amongst rich traders, who from their success are presumed to have sharp and vigorous understandings, and to possess the virtues of diligence, order, constancy, and regularity, and to have cultivated an habitual regard to commutative justice – these are the circumstances of men, that form what I should call a *natural* aristocracy, without which there is no nation.[36]

The French Revolution was nothing less than an attack upon the natural aristocracy in France. The Jacobin movement throughout Europe had for its objective the destruction of the natural aristocracy throughout Europe. The leaders of revolution were 'men of no rank, of no consideration, of wild, savage minds, full of levity, arrogance &

[35] *Works*, V, 432 (*Reflections*).   [36] Ibid., VI, 217–18 (*Appeal*).

presumption, without morals, without probity, without prudence'.[37] These revolutionaries had no stake in any country. They were motivated by envy and by greed. Burke tried to explain how such men had managed to acquire the influence and power which they had:

> In the long series of ages which have furnished the matter of history, never was so beautiful and so august a spectacle presented to the moral eye, as Europe afforded the day before the Revolution in France. I knew indeed that this prosperity contained in itself the seeds of its own danger. In one part of the society it caused laxity and debility; in the other it produced bold spirits and dark designs. A False philosophy passed from academies into courts, and the great themselves were infected with the theories which conducted to their ruin. Knowledge, which in the two last centuries either did not exist at all, or existed solidly on right principles and in chosen hands, was now diffused, weakened, and perverted. General wealth loosened morals, relaxed vigilance, and encreased presumption. Men of talent began to compare, in the partition of the common stock of publick prosperity, the proportions of the dividends with the merits of the claimants. As usual, they found their portion not equal to their estimate (or perhaps to the publick estimate) of their own worth. When it was once discovered by the Revolution in France, that a struggle between establishment and rapacity could be maintained, though but for one year, and in one place, I was sure that a practicable breach was made in the whole order of things and in every country. Religion, that held the materials of the fabric together, was first systematically loosened. All other opinions, under the name of prejudices, must fall along with it, and property, left undefended by principles, became a repository of spoils to tempt cupidity, and not a magazine to furnish arms for defence. I knew, that, attacked on all sides by the infernal energies of talents set in action by vice and disorder, authority could not stand upon authority alone. It wanted some other support than the poise of its own gravity. Situations formerly supported persons. It now became necessary that personal qualities should support situations. Formerly, where authority was found, wisdom and virtue were presumed. But now the veil was torn, and, to keep off sacrilegious intrusion, it was necessary that in the sanctuary of government something should be disclosed not only venerable, but dreadful. Government was at once to shew itself full of virtue and full of force. It was to invite

[37] *Works*, VII, 165 (Remarks on the Policy of the Allies, 1793).

partisans, by making it appear to the world that a generous cause was to be asserted, one fit for a generous people to engage in.[38]

We should not underestimate the extent to which Edmund Burke carefully distinguished the French Revolution from other and earlier revolutions: 'It is a revolt of *innovation*, and thereby the very elements of Society have been confounded and dissipated.'[39] The revolution was an attack upon the basic foundations of European civilization. ('Its spirit lies deep in the corruption of our common nature'.)[40] Burke grimly perceived that Europe stood on the brink of another Dark Age. The false philosophy of the revolution was spreading throughout Europe, sapping its will to resist, undermining the pillars of the old society, releasing the lowest instincts in men. The essence of this disease of Jacobinism was the release of man's basest energies and, unrestrained by religion or by civilization, their harnessing to the Jacobin cause. For Burke, one of the fundamental strengths of Jacobinism was its dangerous appeal to the envy of man.

It is the contempt of Property, and the setting up against its Principle, certain pretended advantages of the State, (which by the way exists only for its conservation) that has led to all the other Evils which have ruined France, and brought all Europe into the most imminent danger. The beginning of the whole mischief was a false Idea, that there is a difference in property according to the description of the persons who hold it under the laws, and the despoiling a Minister of Religion is not the same Robbery with the Pillage of other Men. They, who thro' weakness gave way to the ill designs of bad men in that confiscation, were not long before they practically found their Error. The spoil of the Royal Domaine soon followed the seizure of the Estates of the Church. The appenages of the Kings brothers immediately came on the heels of the usurpation of the Royal Domaine; The Property of the Nobility survived but a short time the appenages of the Princes of the Blood Royal.[41]

Burke took revolutionary France as the prototype Jacobin state founded upon the ending of inequality and the destruction of the natural aristocracy. He did not find its early history attractive, 'Laws overturned; tribunals subverted; industry without vigour; commerce

---

[38] *Works*, VII, 362–4 (Letter to William Elliot, 1795).
[39] Burke to le Chevalier de Rivarol, 1 June 1791, *Correspondence*, VI, 268.
[40] *Works*, VIII, 389 (Second Letter on a Regicide Peace, 1796).
[41] Burke to Comte Mercy-Argentau, *circa* 6 August 1793, *Correspondence*, VI, 389.

expiring; the revenue unpaid, yet the people impoverished; a church pillaged, and a state not relieved; civil and military anarchy make the constitution of the kingdom.'[42] In spite of the considerable amount of rhetorical exaggeration in passages such as this, of one thing Burke was in no doubt: through their insistence upon the philosophy of the rights of man, the Jacobins wished to restructure Europe upon a new basis, rank and heredity counting for nothing, property separated from power, rank from dignity. Jacobinism introduced '*other interests into all countries than those which arose from their locality and natural circumstances*'[43] Power was taken by the Jacobins out of the hands of the natural aristocracy and placed in the hands of 'tradesmen, bankers, and voluntary clubs of bold, presuming young persons; advocates, attornies, notaries, managers of newspapers, and those cabals of literary young men called academics'.[44] This reversal of the natural order of things was typical of Jacobinism. For Jacobinism itself was the reverse of all the customs and norms of civilized life. In particular, Burke thought it a novelty, in all the governments that the world had ever known, for prescription to be regarded as a bar and not as a claim to possession.[45]

In short, then, Jacobinism was a European movement that threatened to reverse the natural order of things and to plunge Europe once more into a Dark Age of anarchy and turbulence. From the historical point of view Burke saw the revolutionary era as the disintegration of Christian Europe. The common, feudal and Christian foundations of European society were the very objects of Jacobinism. Authority and institutions of all kinds were the objects of its attack. Jacobinism weakened authority by constantly assaulting it. The resulting instability was essential to the success of its attack. For Jacobinism itself was the state of social and political instability in which no tie was secure, no authority safe and no order strong enough to prevail.[46] In a Jacobin state like France, Burke saw instability erected into a system. In such a state nothing was constant, nothing was certain. Man's political principles no longer derived from his interests. Political power no longer arose from the ownership of permanent (landed) property. Immediate self-interest was the only public standard for the men who ran the revolution:

'the agitators in corporations . . . societies in the towns formed of directors of assignats, and trustees for the sale of church lands,

[42] *Works*, V, 87-8 (*Reflections*).　　　[43] Ibid., 80.
[44] Ibid., VII, 14, 19 (*Thoughts on French Affairs, 1791*).
[45] Ibid., IX, 64-5 (Fourth Letter on a Regicide Peace, 1797).
[46] Ibid., 58-9.

attornies, agents, money-jobbers, speculators, and adventurers, composing an ignoble oligarchy founded on the destruction of the crown, the nobility and the People'.[47]

The central issue in the struggle, for Burke, was that of religion· The laws and institutions of society stood upon a Christian foundation· The Jacobins' first objective was to weaken and destroy the church; that done, the other institutions of society would collapse in turn.[48] He viewed the war which broke out in Europe in 1792 as nothing less than a war for the survival of religion. Jacobinism was not merely another ideology thrown up by another sect. The French Jacobins had declared 'a war against all sects and all religions'.[49] They were a new species of man, a new breed of political animal, incompatible with the Christian brotherhood of Europe. Their principles represented an attempt to regenerate the moral constitution of man and to condition him in the ideals of the rights of man.[50]

Burke contended, therefore, that the war against the Jacobins must be a crusade on the part of Christian Europe to preserve the independence of nations and the property, liberty and religion of individuals from universal havoc and atheism.[51]

We are in a war of a *peculiar* nature. It is not with an ordinary community, which is hostile or friendly as passion or as interest may veer about, not with a state which makes war through wantonness, and abandons it through lassitude. We are at war with a system, which, by its essence is inimical to all other governments, and which makes peace or war, as peace and war may best contribute to their subversion. It is with an *armed doctrine* that we are at war. It has, by its essence, a faction of opinion, and of interest, and of enthusiasm, in every country. To us it is a Colossus which bestrides our channel. It has one foot on a foreign shore, the other upon the British soil. Thus advantaged, if it can at all exist, it must finally prevail. Nothing can so completely ruin any of the old governments, ours in particular, as the acknowledgement, directly, or by implication, of any kind of superiority in this new power. This acknowledgement we make, if, in a bad or doubtful situation of our affairs, we solicit peace, or if we yield to the modes of new humiliation, in which alone she is content to give us a hearing. By that means the terms cannot be of our choosing, no, not in any part.[52]

[47] *Works*, V, 349 (*Reflections*).   [48] Ibid., 176–82.
[49] Ibid., VII, 175 (Remarks on the Policy of the Allies).
[50] Ibid., VI, 34 (Letter to a Member of the National Assembly).
[51] Ibid., VIII, 236–41 (Second Letter on a Regicide Peace).
[52] Ibid., 98 (First Letter on a Regicide Peace, 1796).

It was, in any case, impossible to make peace with revolutionary France. She considered herself to be outside the public law of Europe, at liberty to pursue her own interests by disrupting the balance of power in Germany and Italy as well as in Europe as a whole.[53] She was determined to destroy the old states of Europe and erect in their place a series of client-states which, through their instability and weakness, would be dependent upon the revolutionary mother-country. 'It is not the Cause of Nation against Nation but . . . the cause of mankind against those who have projected the subversion of that order of things under which our part of the world has so long flourished.'[54] There could, therefore, be no peace with an armed ideology. Every reverse and every setback which the allies suffered in the war confirmed Burke in his belief that to negotiate peace with the regicide republic would be dangerous. Britain should pursue the war with as much vigour as possible. He was never satisfied that a defensive war would be adequate to contain and to destroy Jacobinism.

> . . . we ought, first of all, to be sure, that it is a species of danger, against which any defensive measures, that can be adopted, will be sufficient. Next we ought to know, that the spirit of our laws or that our own dispositions, which are stronger than laws, are susceptible of all those defensive measures, which the occasion may require. A third consideration is, whether these measures will not bring more odium than strength to government; and the last; whether the authority that makes them, in a general corruption of manners and principles, can ensure their execution.[55]

Burke constantly advocated a military strike at Paris and the destruction of Jacobinism once and for all but, as the above quotation suggests, he was, if anything, most of all concerned to safeguard England from revolution. He saw with alarm the proliferation of radical societies and the growing support for French principles even within his own party.[56] He found great cause for concern in 'the irresolution and timidity of the middle sort of men in the country who did nothing to restrain demagogues from their attempts to whip up a popular frenzy and thus things proceed, by a sort of activity of inertness'. Burke gloomily anticipated that the constant proselytizing of the Jacobins at home, together with military reverses abroad, would unsettle the people and

---

[53] *Works*, VIII, 337–9 (Third Letter on a Regicide Peace, 1797).
[54] Burke to Comte Mercy-Argentau, *circa* 6 August 1793, *Correspondence*, VI, 387.
[55] *Works*, IX, 11 (Fourth Letter on a Regicide Peace).
[56] Ibid., VI, 80–5 (*Appeal*).

drain their confidence in the leaders of the country. Popular clamouring for peace would erode the authority of the government, the strength of the legal system and magistracy, and, in turn, allow and encourage the popular spirit to rise even higher. Burke knew that the outcome of the European religious wars against the Jacobins hung upon the survival of England, which in turn depended upon the successful outcome of an aggressive military policy abroad and a united front of the propertied classes at home. Only then could Britain and Europe save themselves from the enemy and launch the counter-revolution against the Jacobins.[57]

Burke saw clearly what the purposes of the counter-revolution should be. He would have nothing to do with the Jacobins. He not only refused to negotiate with them, he would not even allow them to exist. He would not rest until the propertied classes of the *ancien régime* in France had been restored. To that end, the monarchy must be re-established and its property entirely restored, and with it 'the whole fabrick of its ancient laws and usages, political, civil, and religious'. Clearly, the purpose of Burke's counter-revolution was to restore the hereditary, natural aristocracy of the *ancien régime*. In other words, Burke would not allow the Jacobins' seizure of property to start another prescriptive cycle. He wrote on 6 August 1793:

> The people at large in all countries ought to be made sensible that the Symbols of publick Robbery never can have the Sanction and the currency that belong exclusively to the Symbols of publick faith. If any Government should be settled in France upon any other Idea than that of the faithful restitution of all property of all descriptions and that of the rigorous and exemplary punishment of the principal authours and contrivers of its Ruin, I am convinc'd to a certainty, that property, and along with property, Government must fall, (in the same manner in which they have both fallen in France) in every other state in Europe.[58]

'The truth is, that France is out of itself – The moral France is separated from the geographical.'[59] Burke meant that, according to his own principles, the French 'people' no longer existed. For the French to be reconstituted as a people required the re-establishment of her

[57] The passionate conviction which lay behind Burke's fears accounts for the many letters and works which he wrote in the period from 1791 to 1797. These he used to attempt to influence his friends but, more importantly, the ministers. In these attempts he was almost invariable unsuccessful.

[58] Burke to Comte Mercy-Argentau, *circa* 6 August 1793, loc. cit.

[59] *Works*, VII, 139 (Remarks on the Policy of the Allies).

natural aristocracy, her traditional leaders, the emigré aristocracy. Only Frenchmen could recivilize Frenchmen, revive old loyalties and re-establish old institutions. For Burke, then, counter-revolution was *not* a means of obtaining military victory over the French. Such a military victory was only a preliminary, a necessary preliminary, to the re-establishment of French society. The contest, in Burke's mind, was not between Britain and France. It was between legitimate and illegitimate government.

These were the general principles of Burke's counter-revolutionary theory: how to implement counter-revolution was, to a large extent, a matter of circumstance and of necessity. Burke judged that counter-revolution could not generate itself spontaneously from within France. Britain must take 'the directing part' in the anti-French alliance and be 'the soul of the whole confederacy'.[60] Yet the allies must act in concert with the emigrés; they should not impose a settlement upon them. What Burke suggested was that the French nobles of the blood should appoint a regent who should be approved by the *parlements*, then recognized by the allies. This would help to re-establish things 'according to nature and to its fundamental laws'.[61] Thereafter France would have to be liberated and organizations of loyalists – to rival those of the Jacobins – set up. In this context, the church could play a vital role in rallying the people around the standard of the legitimate government of France. Burke was indifferent to the details of the restored regime to be erected in France so long as it was a legitimate government, dedicated to preserving the security of property, for property not numbers, was the basis of government. 'First, therefore, restore property, and afterwards let that property find a government for itself.'[62]

In his counter-revolutionary writings Burke was fond of contrasting the British constitution with that of Jacobin France to establish his thesis that the former rather than the latter most nearly accommodated itself to the nature of man.

> The states of the Christian world have grown up to their present magnitude in a great length of time, and by a great variety of accidents. . . . Not one of them has been formed upon a regular plan

[60] *Works*, VII, 98–104 for Burke's discussion of the counter-revolution inside France. (Heads for Consideration on the Present State of Affairs, 1792.)

[61] For Burke's survey of Europe and his general discussion of the prospects for counter-revolution, see *Works*, VII, 25–46 (*Thoughts on French Affairs*).

[62] Speech on a bill to enable French subjects to enlist in regiments for continental service, 11 April 1794, *Speeches*, IV, 166.

or with any unity of design. As their constitutions are not systematical, they have not been directed to any peculiar end. . . .

The British state is, without question, that which pursues the greatest variety of ends, and is the least disposed to sacrifice any one of them to another, or to the whole. It aims at taking in the entire circle of human desires, and securing for them their fair enjoyment.[63]

It does not follow that Burke recommended other countries to imitate the British system of government. They had their own traditional constitutions which they ought to utilize to their own advantage. The French constitution of the *ancien régime* was well-suited to the French. The representation of estates was the natural and only just representation of France. 'It grew out of the habitual conditions, relations, and reciprocal claims of men. It grew out of the circumstances of the country, and out of the state of property.'[64] While there was a constitution in existence it was the duty of the rulers of the state to govern in accordance with it. In the case of Britain, for example, the constitution derived from three separate principles. Monarchy, aristocracy and democracy must all be supported 'on grounds that are totally different though practically they may be, and happily with us they are, brought into one harmonious body'. He asserted that if only one of the three members was endangered then he would support it to maintain the harmony of the whole.[65]

Burke believed – quite wrongly – that the nature of the British constitution had been unchangeably settled at the time of the Glorious Revolution. He appeared to believe that the Revolution Settlement precluded the possibility of all future change, assuming that the provisions of the legislation of the period bound future parliaments. Furthermore, Burke believed that it was the function of the eighteenth-century aristocracy to defend that constitution and to preserve its benefits by whatever political means might be appropriate – the activities of party, the passage of economical reform legislation or as in the 1790s, the waging of war on revolutionary France. He found nothing inconsistent in his attacks upon the French Revolution in the last decade of the century and his support of the Americans in the 1770s. This was not an admission that rebellion was permissible.

---

[63] Burke's historical account of the background to the *ancien régime* can be found in *Works*, VIII, 253–6 (Second Letter on a Regicide Peace).

[64] Burke discusses the relationship of a representative system to the property structure of a state in *Works*, VI, 56–60 (Letter to a Member of the National Assembly).

[65] Ibid.

Burke believed that the Americans stood 'in the same relation to England, as England did to King James II in 1688' and that they had taken up arms to defend their right to tax themselves 'for the purposes of maintaining civil and military establishments'.[66] Burke proclaimed that his theory of the British constitution, outlined in the *Reflections*, was consistent with the Revolution Settlement, and that what he said in the 1790s was directly derived from the ideology of the Rockingham Whigs.

During the party struggles of the early 1790s Burke was particularly anxious to defend himself from the *New Whigs* in his party who believed that not only the Rockinghams' support of the Americans but their defence also of the Glorious Revolution should have led him to support the French Revolution and the cause of radical reform in Britain. Burke, in fact, thoroughly disapproved of the kind of specious logic used by the 'New Whigs' not only to establish the doctrine of the sovereignty of the people but also to demonstrate 'that in the people the same sovereignty constantly and unalienably resides; that the people may lawfully depose kings, not only for misconduct, but without any misconduct at all'.[67] Burke refuted the opinion that the people may set up and maintain any form of government they chose, that magistracy was not 'a proper subject of contract'.[68] How, then, did Burke succeed in explaining away the Glorious Revolution? Burke argued from the Sachaverell impeachment that

> . . . a breach of the *original contract*, implied and expressed in the constitution of this country, as a scheme of government fundamentally and inviolably fixed in king, lords and commons. – That the fundamental subversion of this ancient constitution, by one of its parts, having been attempted, and in effect accomplished, justified the Revolution. That it was justified *only* upon the *necessity* of the case; as the *only* means left for the recovery of that *ancient* constitution, formed by the *original contract* of the British state: as well as for the future preservation of the same government.[69]

From another point of view, Burke occasionally argued that the Glorious Revolution was designed to preserve property 'guarded by the sacred rules of prescription'. The Glorious Revolution, then, was a revolution *in accordance with* the principle of prescription. The situation of France was different.

With us it was the case of a legal monarch attempting arbitrary

---

[66] *Works*, VI, 123 (*Appeal*).   [67] Ibid., 147.
[68] Ibid.   [69] Ibid., 148.

power – in France it is the case of an arbitrary monarch, beginning from whatever cause, to legalise his authority. The one was to be resisted, the other was to be managed and directed; but in neither case was the order of the state to be changed, lest government might be ruined, which ought only to be corrected and legalized.

The Glorious Revolution, for Burke, was a revolution prevented, not effected, a condition restored, not destroyed.

In the stable fundamental parts of our constitution we made no revolution, no, nor any alteration at all. We did not impair the monarchy.... The nation kept the same ranks, the same orders, the same privileges, the same franchises, the same rules for property, the same subordinations, the same order in the law, in the revenue, and in the magistracy; the same lords, the same Commons, the same corporations, the same electors.[70]

As for France, 'It is a *revolt of innovation*, and thereby the very elements of society have been confounded and dissipated.'[71]

Burke was in no doubt that the most important aspect of the Glorious Revolution had been the restoration of the monarchy 'for without monarchy in England, most certainly we never can enjoy either peace or liberty'.[72] He emphasized the hereditary nature of monarchy, rejecting *New Whig* ideas that the people could choose and cashier their kings. This proposition he defended by referring not merely to the hereditary nature of the British monarchy and to the laws of the land but to the functions of monarchy in society:

Je mesure mon attachement par l'utilité de leurs fonctions jamais augustes et sacrées. Quelles sont ces fonctions? De garder le peuple contre les entreprises des grands, et les grands contre les invasions des peuples, de tenir tout dans sa place et dans son ordre habituel, de consolider l'assemblée, de tout finir dans un sain Milieu, de tout applanir sous l'égalité de la justice et non celui des chimères folles, insolentes, qu'on prêche et qu'on réalise en France.

Conservez l'ordre pour lequel la Monarchie est ordonnée, vous conserverez les Monarques. Permettez la subversion de cet ordre, permettez la magistrature, la prêtrise, la Noblesse, d'être flétries et foulées aux pieds, les monarques et la monarchie périront ensemble.[73]

[70] *Works*, V, 19–20 (Speech on the Army Estimates, 9 February 1790).
[71] Burke to the Comte de Rivarol, 1 June 1791, *Correspondence*, VI, 268.
[72] *Works*, V, 64 (*Reflections*).
[73] Burke to M. de Sandouville, *post*-13 October 1792, ibid., VII, 263.

But hereditary monarchy could not stand unsupported.

> The support of the permanent orders in their places and the re-
> conciling them all to his government, will be his best security, either
> for governing quietly in his own person, or for leaving any sure
> succession to his posterity. Corporations which have a perpetual
> succession, and hereditary nobles who themselves exist by Succession
> are the true guardians of Monarchical succession. On such orders
> and institutions alone an hereditary monarch can stand.[74]

The relationship between monarchy and aristocracy was particularly
important. 'In a monarchy the aristocracy must ever be nearer to the
crown than to the democracy, because it originated in the crown as the
fountain of honour'.[75] The aristocracy, he had learned from the French
experience, was the first line of defence for the monarchy. Early in
1792 he wrote:

> The name of the Monarchy, and of the hereditary monarchy too,
> they preserve in France, and they feed the person whom they call
> King, with such a Revenue, given to mere luxury and extravagance,
> totally separated from all provision for the State, as, I believe, no
> people ever before dreamed of granting for such purposes. But
> against the Nobility and Gentry they have waged inexpiable War.
> There are, at this day, no fewer than ten thousand heads of respect-
> able families driven out of France; and those who remain at home,
> remain in depression, penury, and continual alarm for their Lives.[76]

All of these crimes had been undertaken by and on behalf of 'the
people'. Running through all of Burke's revolutionary thought is the
assumption that the people have no right to political power. This is a
strain of thought which went back to the earliest days of his political
career. He never tired of making the point that government, far from
being a matter of arithmetic, was a delicate and sophisticated proceeding,
requiring the understanding of the total political situation in its many
aspects and their prudential management, not blind subservience to
public opinion. The politician must listen to the popular voice but
he must not be led by it. His duty was to maintain the constitution
and the establishments of the state. The principle that political power
should be exercised on behalf of the people and in the public interest
was not at all the same thing as slavishly following the cries of the
mob. The politician had his responsibilities to the people but he also

[74] Burke to Rivarol, 1 June 1791, loc. cit.
[75] Speech on the Quebec Act, 11 May 1791, *Speeches*, IV, 32.
[76] Burke to William Weddell, 31 January 1792, loc. cit.

had his responsibilities to God.[77] Burke did not rule out the possibility that 'There may be situations in which the purely democratic form will become necessary', but there is little doubt that these cases he regarded as exceptional. Of those who, parrot-like, chanted the contemporary catch phrases about popular power, Burke asked:

> Have they never heard of a monarchy, directed by laws, controlled and balanced by the great hereditary wealth and hereditary dignity of a nation, and both again controlled by a judicious check from the reason and feeling of the people at large acting by a suitable and permanent organ?[78]

Burke had a clear conception of the deferential attitudes of the people in his ideal polity: 'They must respect that property of which they cannot partake. They must labour to obtain what by labour can be obtained.'[79] For Burke, 'The tyranny of a multitude is a multiplied tyranny', as the French Revolution illustrated perfectly clearly.[80] For in France the people were not their own masters. They were, therefore, easily corruptible and easily controllable, through flattery, through lavish promises and through demagoguery. As he wrote in *The Appeal*: 'The pretended *rights of men* . . . cannot be the rights of the people. For to be a people, and to have these rights, are things incompatible. The one supposes the presence, the other the absence, of a state of civil society.'[81] In many of the later works, Burke argued directly against proposals to extend the franchise. His most famous argument against it was his computation that only about 400,000 people at the most should enjoy the franchise, 'those of adult age, not declining in life, of tolerable leisure for such discussions, & of some means of information'.[82] If men did not deserve the vote, their opinions on the issues of the day could safely be neglected. In any case, in constitutional theory, the problem did not arise. For parliament was infallible when it came to collecting the sentiments of the people.

> In legal construction, the sense of the people of England is to be collected from the house of Commons, and, though I do not deny the possibility of an abuse of this trust as well as any other, yet I

[77] Burke discusses the moral duties of political leaders in *Works*, V, 176–8 (*Reflections*).
[78] Ibid., 229.   [79] Ibid., 429.
[80] Burke to Captain Thomas Mercer, 26 February 1790, *Correspondence*, VI, 96.
[81] Burke's principal discussion of natural rights is in *Works*, VI, 208–15, *passim* (*Appeal*).
[82] Ibid., VIII, 140–1 (First Letter on a Regicide Peace).

think, that without the most weighty reasons, and in the most urgent exigencies, it is highly dangerous to suppose that the house speaks any thing contrary to the sense of the people, or that the representative is silent when the sense of the constituent, strongly, decidely, and upon long deliberation, speaks audibly upon any topick of moment. If there is a doubt, whether the house of commons represents perfectly the whole commons of Great Britain, (I think there is none) there can be no question but that the lords and the commons together represent the sense of the whole people to the Crown, and to the world. Thus it is, when we speak legally and constitutionally. In a great measure, it is equally true, when we speak prudentially; but I do not pretend to assert, that there are no other principles to guide discretion than those which are or can be fixed by some law, or some constitution; yet before the legally presumed sense of the people should be superseded by a supposition of one more real, (as in all cases, where a legal presumption is to be ascertained,) some strong proofs ought to exist of a contrary disposition in the people at large, and some decisive indications of their desire upon this subject.[83]

His suspicion of popular sovereignty did not mean that Burke was in any way opposed to popular liberty. As we have seen, he rejected the French version: 'It was a liberty without property, without honour, without morals, without order, without government, without security of life. In order to gain liberty they had forfeited order, and had thus forfeited every degree of freedom.'[84] Burke contrasted French liberty with the defence of liberty undertaken in England at the Glorious Revolution. As in the 1770s, Burke understood liberty to be a consequence of civil order and personal restraint. It was not to be taken as the theoretical foundation of government, 'The Revolution was made to preserve our *antient* indisputable laws and liberties, and that *antient* constitution of government which is our only security for law and liberty.'[85] He had no faith in unrestricted liberty: 'But what is liberty without wisdom, and without virtue? It is the greatest of all possible evils; for it is folly, vice, and madness, without tuition or restraint.' It was the easiest thing in the world to remove restraint but it was much more difficult to establish free government, 'that is, to temper together these opposite elements of liberty and restraint in one consistent work'.[86] Not that liberty was only for a few:

I certainly think that all Men who desire it, deserve it. It is not the

---

[83] *Works*, VIII, 323-4 (Third Letter on a Regicide Peace).
[84] See above, p. 110.   [85] *Works*, V, 74 (*Reflections*).   [86] Ibid., 434.

Reward of our Merit or the acquisition of our Industry. It is our Inheritance. It is the birthright of our Species. We cannot forfeit our right to it, but by what forfeits our title to the privileges of our kind; I mean the abuse or oblivion of our rational faculties, and a ferocious indocility.[87]

Burke's liberty has nothing to do with political power or with economic equality. Burke's ordered liberty is the freedom of every man to enjoy the natural rights of social, civilized life.

No account of Burke's later philosophy is complete without some discussion of the place occupied by religion in the corpus of his revolutionary thought. That place is by no means as straightforward as some modern commentators have maintained. Burke himself confessed that the workings of Divine Providence in history were beyond man's understanding and he admitted that he saw no discernible patterns in the history of civilizations.

> It is often impossible, in these political enquiries, to find any proportion between the apparent force of any moral causes we may assign and their known operation. We are therefore obliged to deliver up that operation to mere chance, or, more piously, (perhaps more rationally,) to the occasional interposition and irresistible hand of the Great Disposer. We have seen states of considerable duration, which for ages have remained nearly as they have begun, and could hardly be said to ebb or flow. Some appear to have spent their vigour at their commencement. Some have blazed out in their glory a little before their extinction. The meridian of some has been the most splendid. Others, and they the greatest number, have fluctuated, and experienced at different periods of their existence a great variety of fortune. At the very moment when some of them seemed plunged in unfathomable abysses of disgrace and disaster, they have suddenly emerged. They have begun a new course and opened a new reckoning; and, even in the depths of their calamity, and on the very ruins of their country, have laid the foundations of a towering and durable greatness. All this has happened without any apparent previous change in the general circumstances which had brought on their distress. The death of a man at a critical juncture, his disgust, his retreat, his disgrace, have brought innumerable calamities on a whole nation. A common soldier, a child, a girl at the door of an inn, have changed the face of fortune, and almost of nature.[88]

[87] Burke to Depont, November 1789, loc. cit.
[88] *Works*, VIII, 79–80 (First Letter on a Regicide Peace).

Furthermore, in spite of his strong religious convictions and his frequent appeals to the Divine Providence, towards the end of his life Burke began to despair of the future of European culture, civilization and Christianity. Burke could not begin to understand the cosmic reasons why God was prepared to leave man to the mercy of the Jacobins. If the French Revolution was an atheistic attack upon Christianity, then why did God allow it to succeed ? Burke did not have satisfactory answers to these questions and went to his grave a bewildered and demoralized man, believing that the curfew of European civilization had been sounded. From the very beginning, he had regarded the French Revolution as a profanity, an atheistic assault upon the sacred principles of Christianity, an infection of the moral order by the rationalistic individualism of the Enlightenment which attacked the basic units of society, the family, the church, the community and the corporate institutions of the nation. How Burke's God could permit the disruption of society and the destruction of the church of Christ, his means of maintaining virtue, morality and order in the world of man, is a question which takes us to the very limits of our knowledge of Burke's philosophy.

Only on rare occasions did Burke allow such insoluble problems to distract him from more practical considerations. His primary concern with religion was with its social and political manifestations. Burke always believed that politics could never be separated from morality and that political rights and duties required a moral justification. Furthermore Burke was aware of the 'benefits which society in general derived from the morality founded upon the belief of the existence of a God, and the comforts which individuals felt in leaving this world, in the hope of enjoying happiness in the next'.[89] It was scarcely surprising if Burke defended strongly the religious establishments then under attack from radical reformers.

Church establishments for Burke fulfilled several important functions in the life of the state. They acted as the vehicle of man's religious awareness, 'the first of our prejudices, not a prejudice destitute of reason, but involved in a profound and extensive reason. It is first, and last, and midst in our minds'.[90] Furthermore, they placed before the governors of a state 'high and worthy notions of their function and destination'.[91] It also operated 'with an wholesome awe upon free citizens' in that it impressed upon them the notion that power was a *trust*.[92] The Church of England was in an anomalous position with respect to the state, attached to it, but in many ways, independent of it. It was not an organ of the state but one of the largest independent

[89] *Works*, VIII, 81–2.   [90] Ibid., V, 176 (*Reflections*).   [91] Ibid.   [92] Ibid.

owners of landed property in the country.[93] Attacks upon the church, therefore, became attacks upon the whole social order. Church and state were inextricably bound up together in their struggle for survival in civil society. The example of France persuaded Burke that under the pretence of reform the whole church could be brought crashing down and after it the civil institutions which buttressed the fabric of the state. Naturally, then, in Burke's later thought, there occurred a gradual but noticeable shift in the direction of strengthening the powers and rights of the state at the expense of the degree of individual dissent which Burke had earlier been prepared to allow. He laid it down that 'government, representing the society, has a general superintending control over all the actions, and over all the publicly propagated doctrines of men'. Therefore, 'A reasonable, prudent, provident and moderate coercion, may be a means of preventing acts of extreme ferocity and rigour.'[94] It would be mistaken to assume that Burke believed in an *alliance* between church and state. He was too Erastian to make such an assumption.

> An alliance is between two things that are in their nature distinct and independent, such as between two sovereign states. But in a Christian commonwealth the church and state are one and the same thing, being different, integral parts of the same whole.

Therefore the Christian magistrate must concern himself with religious affairs and opinions. 'As religion is one of the bonds of society, he ought not to suffer it to be made the pretext of destroying its peace, order, liberty, and its security.'[95] There is no doubt that Burke believed a careless and casual toleration of religious opinions which were fundamentally different to those entertained by most British people to be a dangerous mistake. He warned: 'we have consecrated the state, that no man should approach to look into its defects or corruptions but with due caution; that he should never dream of beginning its reformation by its subversion'.[96] Therefore, 'He who gave our nature to be perfected by our virtue, willed also the necessary means of its perfection – He willed therefore the state – He willed its connexion with the source and original archetype of all perfection.'[97] As the state and its coercive power come to occupy a larger place in his political thinking, then, the

---

[93] A point which Burke chooses to ignore.
[94] Speech on the Catholic Dissenters' Relief Bill, 1 March 1791, *Speeches*, III, 543.
[95] Speech on the Unitarians' Petition, 11 May 1792, ibid., IV, 55–7.
[96] *Works*, V, 183 (*Reflections*).   [97] Ibid., 186.

emphasis which he had earlier placed upon individual rights diminished.

In the 1790s, therefore, Burke perceptibly changed his ground on the question of toleration for Dissenters. He identified their doctrine indiscriminately with the principles of democracy, accusing them of wishing to imitate the French Revolution. Although the Dissenters' view of the state was different to that of Burke (that is, their notion of the voluntary congregation contrasted with his conception of the hereditary corporation in a close relationship with the state) it was ridiculous for him seriously to charge them with plotting the downfall of church and state. Occasionally Burke would make an example of the statements of certain dissenting ministers, only to plunge himself into some terrible logical and theological tangles. On one occasion, in attempting to refute the view that the state had no right of coercion over the beliefs of individuals, his didactical method led him to the remarkable conclusion that the state 'had an uncontrollable super-intending power over those opinions, and it was highly necessary for the prosperity, the safety, the good morals, and the happiness of the community, that it should have such a power'.[98] It was tragic that the crisis of the church and state in the 1790s should have made into an unbridgeable chasm of opinion a difference of view which Burke had formerly been well prepared to tolerate. It was with anger and horror that Burke refuted the Dissenters' belief that toleration and relief were rights and not privileges. (The right to hold dissenting opinions was emphatically *not* one of Burke's natural rights.) He regarded the church-state not as a voluntary association but as a corporate entity, imposing uniformity in most essentials. He rejected all thought of further relief for the Dissenters because in the conditions of the 1790s he had come to identify religious dissent with political subversion.

Edmund Burke's state in the 1790s was not an open society. It was an embattled castle with Dissenters swarming at the gates. Burke found it impossible to comply with their demands.

As long as they continue to claim what they desire as a *Right*; so long will they find it difficult to obtain it. Parliament will not hear of an *abstract principle*, which must render it impossible to annexe any qualification Whatsoever to the capacity of exercising a publick Trust; and I am myself much of the same Mind; though I would have these qualifications as few and as moderate as possible. This high claim of *Right*, leaves with Parliament no *discretionary* power whatsoever concerning almost any part of *Legislation*, which is almost all of it, conversant in qualifying and limiting some *Right or*

---

[98] Speech on the Catholic Dissenters Relief Bill, loc. cit.

other of man's original nature. As long as principal Leading men among the dissenters make *Associations* on this *Subject*; so long will they keep up the general Alarm. As long as they shew, not a cool, temperate, conscientious dissent, but a warm, animated and acrimonious Hostility against the Church establishment, and by all their words and actions manifest a settled design of subverting it, so long will they, in my poor opinion, be met, in any attempt whatsoever of the least consequence, with a decided opposition.[99]

Burke really believed that nine tenths of the Dissenters were 'entirely devoted, some with greater some with less zeal, to the principles of the French Revolution', more dangerous than the Jacobites of the eighteenth or the republicans of the seventeenth century.

For my part, I shall never think that a party, of at least seven hundred thousand souls, with such recruits as they can pick up, in this Kingdom, and with a body united with them in Sentiments and principles, and more susceptible of violent passions, can be in the present state of things, a ground, upon which one can rest in perfect Security. A foreign factious connexion is the very essence of their politicks. Their Object is avowedly to abolish all national distinctions and local interests and prejudices, and to merge them all in one Interest and one Cause, which they call the rights of man. They wish to break down all Barriers which tend to separate them from the Counsels, designs, and assistance, of the republican, atheistical, faction of Fanaticks in France. France, in the very plenitude of any power which she possessed in this Century, would be no Object of serious alarm to England, if she had no connexion with parties in this Kingdom. With a connexion here which considers the predominant power in France as their natural friend and ally, I should think Three of four departments in Normandy more formidable than the whole of that once great Monarchy. At this moment I think, There is no danger from them. But our danger must be from our not looking beyond the moment.[100]

Burke's earlier Whig theories of limited government tended to give way in the 1790s to an emphasis on the powers of state. In 1772, he had considered the will of the majority to be an important consideration in his discussions of toleration. Twenty years later it was of no account at all. He was less concerned with the merits of toleration than with the *consequences* of toleration.

[99] Burke to John Noble, 14 March 1790, *Correspondence*, VI, 100–4.
[100] Burke to Henry Dundas, 30 September 1791, ibid., 418–22.

The Burke who in his early career had admitted only moderate, restorative reform for an immediate purpose and a predictable end threw up his hands in horror when he thought he saw the bastions of European order crumbling. His reaction was emotive and hysterical, his analysis of events superficial and rhetorical. For example, his account of the *ancien régime* in France scarcely mentioned those economic and social aspects of the kingdom of Louis XVI which, in the end, destroyed both him and it. Like all alarmists, Burke ascribed evil events to evil men and evil ideas. There is considerable truth – perhaps more than many of Burke's admirers concede – in the charge that Burke viewed events from above and that he acquired a partisan view of the situation. For example, it never seems to have occurred to him to inquire into the astonishingly widespread *acquiescence* in the revolution in France. Furthermore, his continued support for a bankrupt monarchy was as astonishing as it was pertinacious, his lacrimonious sympathy for the privileged orders who had persistently and selfishly refused to permit any diminution of their enormous privileges astounding. Equally unrealistic was his sublimely peaceful view of British history. He completely ignored the Civil War and skated rapidly over the frequent outbreaks of religious and political instability in Tudor, Stuart and early Hanoverian England. His abandonment of most of the humanitarian reforms which he had previously espoused was regrettable. His earlier, real, if cautious, meliorism degenerated into a superficial fear of the mob. He continued to accept the divine right of the aristocracy to run not only Britain but every part of Europe without pausing for a moment to consider to what extent they had been, were, or would be fit to do so. He had more sympathy for the minor deprivations of a few aristocratic French families than he had for the sufferings of the poor of Europe. His willingness not only to tolerate, approve, but also applaud the existence of inequality was narrow-minded in the age of Rousseau. His willingness to tolerate any abuse in a working political system was curiously dated in the age of the enlightened despots. It is not that Burke's expediency made him short-sighted. Indeed, his expediency has been much exaggerated. The clue to the shortcomings of his political philosophy perhaps follow from his *method*. His style of arguing didactically from one subject to a pre-determined conclusion was essentially that of the politician rather than the philosopher of the state. As a man of affairs, deeply and politically concerned in the issues with which he dealt, Burke was able to take neither a detached and broad view nor adopt a sober, historical assessment in any of his campaigns and crusades. But one further thing may yet be said about

Burke's revolutionary thought. There was room for a critic of the revolution in the Europe of the 1790s. Burke was not that critic. He lacked the detachment to fill that role. Burke rejected the new order entirely, from its supposed ideological origins to its allegedly disastrous consequences. The revolutionary thought of Edmund Burke offered neither an analytical interpretation nor a critical rebuttal of the ideals of the French Revolution. In the last analysis, he was mainly concerned to argue the revolution out of existence.

CONCLUSION

Edmund Burke was a philosopher of an unusual kind. He believed that political philosophy had, at best, a modest function to perform in the life of society. Political philosophy defined questions; it could not solve problems. Nevertheless, Burke saw an inseparable relationship between politics and philosophy. Without the latter, the former would degenerate into a meaningless expediency. His conception of the limited function of political philosophy arose, perhaps, from Burke's view of man. Burke believed in the essential weakness and corruptibility of human nature, in the incapacity of the average man to resolve his problems in a rational manner, in the irrelevance of most 'rational' solutions to political problems, in the dangers inherent in most forms of political activism, especially those radical experiments with existing institutions which might cause unforeseeable damage. Edmund Burke's conservatism arose, therefore, directly from one of the most fundamental assumptions in his thought. Indeed, it was a function of his own political philosophy to defend the established order of things.

Burke's conservatism was also to a considerable extent conditioned by his philosophical method. This can be described in many ways and by many words but perhaps few would incline to dispute the assertion that Burke's method was *practical*. His practical involvement in party politics, his first-hand experience of public life, his familiarity with Ireland, and also, to a point, with France, the energy which he expended in mastering the details of colonial America, revolutionary France and Warren Hastings' India – all these provide an impressive factual and practical basis for his political philosophy. Paradoxically, it was the fact that Burke was such an accomplished expert in many of the affairs of his time which helped to make him so conservative. His detailed knowledge of affairs revealed to him the true complexities of political situations and political problems together with the irrelevance of so many of the nostrums of the right and the left. His political preoccupations served to orientate Burke's interests and to direct his attention to the present and to divert him from the past. To some extent, at least, this was why he was uninterested in origins and precedents. It was characteristic of Burke, for example, to defend the owners of present property and to neglect to inquire into their title to ownership by investigating how they obtained it.

His method is also didactic and rhetorical. Not for Burke the calm, detached 'philosophical' discussion. Burke's political philosophy *is* the philosophy of the politician. It was evolved in the press and on the floor of the House of Commons, in public and in party. His political philosophy is the disputation of a public figure constantly engaged in controversy and conflict. His inquiries, it goes without saying, were not intended to be academic treatises. They were directed towards the solution of certain pressing political problems not towards explaining the workings of society or the operation of the Divine Providence. He is uninterested, therefore, in establishing the truth of general conclusions from his investigations although he occasionally found it useful to buttress his practical suggestions with the fruitful generalizations which he was able to extract from almost any political or historical situation. It is, consequently futile to argue about Burke's consistency. As a practical politician, Burke was consistent or inconsistent depending upon the level at which commentators choose to pitch their inquiries and to define the words they use. It does not seem to be particularly fruitful to demand whether Burke retracted or adhered to his early ideas and opinions. *He moved on.* He moved on to different areas of political conflict and to fresh conflicts of principles. The most consistent thing about Burke's political philosophy, indeed, was not one or other of his 'theories' but his philosophical method.

That method was, perhaps, best displayed in Burke's contribution to the American problem. As we have seen, his thought kept pace with events and his ideas were always directed towards remedying some situation. Burke was well aware of the legacy of the past and its significance in political disputes but he utilized that awareness to assist his understanding of the colonial problem. Characteristically, he assumed that there was nothing basically wrong with existing institutions, consoling himself with the sanguine feeling that new men and fresh attitudes were all that were needed to reduce the political temperature and to solve all problems. Hence he wished to understand the human factor in the American situation and went to some trouble to familiarize himself with those environmental influences which had conditioned the spirit of liberty in America. His characteristic lack of interest in rights and their enforcement reflected his belief that man rather than his institutions was the primary agent in the historical process. In exactly the same way, on Irish affairs he thought it more important to remedy the grievance felt by the Irish people than to assert the legislative sovereignty of the British parliament for its own sake.

As we remarked earlier, Burke's ability to eschew a legalistic approach to politics was one of the most refreshing and most original aspects of his approach to statecraft. Yet, in other ways, his philosophy – even its most basic assumptions – amounted to little more than an unthinking acceptance and reiteration of some of the traditional themes of political and intellectual life which had become embedded in the European consciousness. His horror of corruption he derived, no doubt, from the classical authors whom he read in his youth. To the idea of corruption he closely related the Machiavellian idea of the balance of the three constituent parts of the constitution (monarchy, aristocracy and democracy). Burke, like so many of his contemporaries, believed that if one of the three became too powerful, then, the balance of the constitution would be upset. This unsettling of the constitution could only occur if the 'independence' of any part of it were infringed; such an infringement could only occur through corruption. That was not the end of the matter, for the constitutional dislocation of a state would be followed, gradually but inexorably, by the wholesale corruption of the people which, in turn, would lead to the overthrow of the state. Like many of his contemporaries, Burke blindly accepted assumptions such as these. Essentially, men of his generation were afraid of power. Political philosophy was devoted to discussing how to limit it rather than how to use it. Yet from these simple assumptions of an ancient European tradition so much in Burke's career followed. The conception of party, for example, was connected to Burke's wish to re-establish the independence of the British parliament. Party not only cured 'Discontents'; it also safeguarded the independence of the individual member. Party was thus one of Burke's suggestions for dealing with the eternal problem of corruption.

In the same way, he adopted an idea that was common to practically all thinkers and writers of the eighteenth century. This was the ideal of *restoration*, the notion that the ideal towards which politicians ought to address themselves was not some future utopia but the revival of a Golden Age and the re-application of its principles to a contemporary situation. We have already seen how powerfully this belief moved Burke, not only in his party thought but in his more general theories of the British constitution and also in his attitudes towards the empire, especially Ireland and America. This ideal was, of course, a metaphysical, not an historical assumption. Politics, for Burke's generation in Britain, did not concern 'progress'. It was concerned with an ancient cycle of renewal, restoration, corruption, decay, disintegration and, once more, renewal.

Underpinning Edmund Burke's political philosophy, then, was a mentality which rendered coherent the diverse and seemingly unconnected experiences of his career. The influence of Lord Bute and the spreading of corruption from the British court were no different, when all was said and done, from the corruption exported to India by the East India Company and practised by Warren Hastings. This, in its turn, was merely a manifestation of the same force for evil as the corrupt operations of the Protestant Ascendancy in Ireland. Burke's *remedies* to all these problems differed according to the situation. The *problem*, however, was fundamentally the same in all these cases.

It is within considerations such as these that the interpretation of Burke's thought must proceed. Not that Burke followed the unstated assumptions of his age invariably. As we have observed, he injected new elements into the sterile Whiggism of the mid-eighteenth century. In converting Whiggism into the ideology of opposition he laid particular emphasis upon the popular nature of politics and the public responsibilities of those who govern. He redefined Whiggism in a novel, prescriptive manner which still left room for reform (albeit restorative), the protection of liberty and the extension of toleration. Late in his career, however, Burke found it necessary to lay emphasis not upon the progressive ideas of the day but upon the fundamental units of society whose existence he sincerely believed to be endangered. His thought became directed towards justifying the social purpose of the state, of property, of government, of monarchy, of aristocracy and of the church establishment. The *conclusions* which Burke reached during the 1790s were not in their general direction inconsistent with those he had reached earlier in his career. The events of that decade only served to confirm Burke's belief that political change best operated when it restored the state to its original nature. The 1790s, in short, reinforced strongly the conservatism which was already such a marked feature of his political philosophy and elicited a more substantial, more theoretical and more soundly philosophically based statement of it than Burke had hitherto made.

During his final years the philosopher of restorative Whiggism propounded a philosophy of conservation which many commentators have too hastily identified with Conservatism. It may readily be conceded that Burke's political philosophy both made Conservatism possible and paved the way for its ultimate expression in the decades after his death. Burke's political philosophy, it may be said, acts as a bridge between the restorative Whiggism which dominated the English mind in the middle and later eighteenth century and the Romantic Conservatism of the early nineteenth. There can be no doubt that his attack upon the political philosophies of the Enlightenment and of the English Dissenters challenged the status which 'reason' had enjoyed in European thought for over half a century. His assertion of the importance of custom, of habit and of instinct in the life of man and of society drastically curtailed the realm of reason. For Burke, both men and societies were too complex and too delicate to lend themselves to the sophisticated yet superficial generalizings of the Philosophes. Burke was horrified at the effects upon society of the proliferation of Enlightenment rationalism; in particular, he deplored its subversive effects upon the basic units of civilized, social life, the family, the church and the state. Burke's 'conservatism' consists of far more, however, than the recognition of the importance of 'non-rational' considerations in society. Burke perceived the universality of change in human history and the transience of the present. He trembled on the verge of an organic view of social life which observed societies as living things with a past and a future contained within a historical world of continuity. Yet Burke, while he caught an early glimpse of the organic notion of the state, lacked a perspective on the future which the organic theory, in its fully developed form, demanded. Burke was so anxious to preserve the fruits of the past in the present that he was unable to look to the future. Burke rejected the Enlightenment's characteristic idea of progress because of his pessimism concerning man's capabilities to organize society upon a basis of controlled and progressive reform. In this sense, too, then, Burke's Political Philosophy is a bridge between restorative Whiggery and the Romantic movement.

All such labels are, however, of very limited use. They may help to suggest ideas and to establish relationships between thinkers and schools but they probably do more harm than good. Burke was an idiosyncratic figure in his time. He is impossible to label. It is wiser to understand why this is so than to fail to resist the temptation to apply a label to him. He rejected many aspects of the Whiggism of Locke but even more of the radical thought of men like Burgh, Cartwright and Paine. In some ways Burke was an unusual figure for the eighteenth century for he explicitly and powerfully rejected many of its most fundamental ideas. He detested its intense legalism and its preoccupation with precedent. He almost entirely ignored its idea of the unchanging nature of man. He rejected its simplistic belief in progress. He refuted the existence of its idyllic 'state of nature' in which free men peacefully nodded their assent to the contract. He disagreed with the widespread view that men were rational and independent agents capable of pursuing rational courses of action. He accepted only with severe reservations the opinion that man had 'natural rights' which it was the function of the state to preserve. In spite of his conservatism, then, Burke cast aside several of the fetters which had for long restricted the development of political philosophy. He succeeded in breaking new ground and in opening up new problems for investigation. Edmund Burke not merely made a contribution to the development of political philosophy but, in a very real sense, succeeded in extending its horizons and in enlarging its province.

BIBLIOGRAPHY

During the 'Burke Revival' of the last two decades an enormous amount of material on Burke has been published. Only a small portion of it, however, can be recommended with any enthusiasm.

On Burke's life:

The older biographies are now out of date in their general political interpretation but R. Murray's *Edmund Burke* (1931), and Sir Philip Magnus's *Edmund Burke: A Life* (1939) retain some value as readable and balanced accounts of their subject. Carl B. Cone's *Burke and the Nature of Politics* (2 vols, University of Kentucky Press, 1957, 1964) is a detailed and ambitious work. Although we are fortunate to have a scholarly, modern biography of Burke, Cone is rather uncritical of his subject and somewhat superficial in his treatment of the politics of Burke's times. On certain aspects of his career Burke has been well served. T. H. D. Mahoney's *Edmund Burke and Ireland* (Harvard, 1960) collects together most of the relevant material in a competent manner. N. C. Phillips, 'Edmund Burke and the County Movement', *English Historical Review* (1961), discusses a significant turning point in his career while P. J. Marshall, *The Impeachment of Warren Hastings* (Oxford, 1965), reaches standards of scholarship and impartiality which Burke studies badly need. On many issues, however, the reader can only be advised to read of Burke's day to day involvement in politics in his *Correspondence* (general editor, T. Copeland) and to read his *Works*.

Philosophy

The 'New Conservative' interpretation of Burke's philosophy with its concentration upon the Natural Law has been the most powerful vehicle for Burke studies since the last war. This interpretation has not been accepted in England although in America it continues to colour much that is written on Burke. It owed much to Leo Strauss, *Natural Right and History* (Chicago, 1953), and Russell Kirk, *The Conservative Mind from Burke to Santayana* (New York, 1953). The Introduction to R. Hoffman and P. Levack (eds), *Burke's Politics* (New York, 1949), is an early – and extreme – anticipation of the Natural Law interpretation. For statements of the Natural Law school see Russell Kirk, 'Burke and Natural Rights', *The Review of Politics*, XIII (1951), the more moderate and far more compelling essay by Charles Parkin, *The Moral Basis of Burke's Political Thought* (Cambridge, 1956), and the most complete discussion of the subject by Peter Stanlis, *Edmund Burke and the Natural Law* (Ann Arbor, Michigan, 1958). F. Canavan, *The Political Reason of Edmund Burke* (Durham, North Carolina, 1960) is an influential and interesting discussion. The Natural Law interpretation was qualified rather than criticized by B. T. Wilkins, *The Problem of Burke's Political Philosophy* (Oxford, 1967).

An alternative – and far more convincing – approach to Burke's philosophy is to attempt to understand what Burke really meant and to explain the concepts which he used. This had been patchily done and no 'interpretation' of Burke's philosophy as such exists. What could be done is dazzlingly illustrated by J. G. A. Pocock's masterful 'Burke and the Ancient Constitution', *Historical Journal*, III (1960). Pocock stresses Burke's debt to the Common Law tradition of the previous century but makes no claim that Burke can *only* be understood in these terms. C. P. Courtenay's, *Montesquieu and Burke* (Oxford, 1963), is in many ways a similar reassertion of Burke's traditionalist outlook. (For the beginner, indeed, Courtenay offers perhaps the best brief introduction to Burke's philosophy that exists.)

Particular aspects of Burke's philosophy have been adequately dealt with as follows: A. M. Osborn *Rousseau and Burke* (1940); R. Fennessy, *Burke, Paine and the Rights of Man* (The Hague, 1963); Harvey Mansfield Jnr, *Statesmanship and Party Government* (Chicago, 1965) is a controversial though brilliant example of a philosophical analysis of Burke's thought. Burke's idea of prescription has been perceptively and engagingly dealt with by Paul Lucas, 'On Edmund Burke's Doctrine of Prescription; Or, An Appeal from the New to the Old Lawyers', *Historical Journal*, XI (1968). Lucas breaks new ground in this article and opens the way towards an effective synthesis of Burke's ideas of History, Change and Prescription.

INDEX